THE HERMIT
AND OTHER ZEN TALES

with Commentaries by
HENRY B. PLATOV

Translated from the German by
Michelle Bromley

The Hermit and other Zen Tales
With Commentaries by Henry B. Platov

Copyright © for the English edition, Michelle Bromley 2025

Originally published in German as Der Eremit und andere
Zen Erzählungen, 1989

Published with the support of Hokun Trust in association
with The Buddhist Society

Funded by The Hokun Trust
Charity No: 1129031

Publisher: BoD · Books on Demand GmbH,
Überseering 33, 22297 Hamburg, bod@bod.de
Print: Libri Plureos GmbH, Friedensallee 273,
22763 Hamburg
ISBN: 978-3-7693-2573-7

Edited by Michelle Bromley
Designed by Sandra Hill

Cover image: Xianzi, the 'Shrimp Eater', Kano Tan'yu, 17th c.

Hokun Trust
58 Marlborough Place
London NW8 0PL
Email: thehokuntrust@gmail.com
www.hokun-trust.org

THE HERMIT
AND OTHER ZEN TALES

with Commentaries by
HENRY B. PLATOV

Fragrance
of the
Dharma
Hōkun Trust

THE BUDDHIST SOCIETY TRUST

Fragrance
of the
Dharma
Hōkun Trust

The Hokun Trust is pleased to support this volume of
The Hermit and Other Zen Tales
with Commentaries by Henry B. Platov

CONTENTS

PREFACE TO THE ENGLISH EDITION

This little book, *The Hermit and other Zen Tales*, is a collection of Dharma talks (*teisho*) given by the late Zen teacher H. B. Platov, Chikuen Kugai (1904-1990). The text on which these commentaries are based is *The Tales of Tokuzan* by W. J. Gabb. Tokuzan is a fictional Zen master created by Gabb and these engaging tales of the encounters between a Zen master and his monks in the Tang dynasty aptly capture the spirit of Zen and provided the springboard for Platov's insightful and inspiring commentaries. With his deep roots in Zen, H. B. Platov discusses many aspects of Zen training and from his rich cultural background he draws on analogies from the traditions of the great world religions, as well as from philosophy and psychology, emphasising the aspirations that are common to the human spirit everywhere and throughout time.

I was first introduced to this book many years ago when I was given a copy by my teacher, Ven. Myokyo-ni. I was immediately taken by the engaging stories of Tokuzan and inspired by Platov's wonderful and thought-provoking commentaries. But beyond this, something else struck a chord, there was a strong sense of familiarity with the book and its author. When I mentioned this to Myokyo-ni, she nodded and smiled, acknowledging that this was only natural since Sokei-an Sasaki was Dr. Platov's teacher and her own teacher was Oda Sesso Roshi, so there was a shared Zen lineage.

I always found it disappointing that this wonderful book was only available in German and was therefore pleased when Ven. Agetsu

Wydler of the Zentrum für Zen Buddhismus in Zürich welcomed an English translation and that the Hokun Trust and The Buddhist Society have agreed to bring it out. Thus, the book almost seems to have completed a full circle, as it is returning to where it started with Gabb's Tales, but has along the way grown and acquired another dimension with Dr. Platov's commentaries. Hopefully it will now embark on a new journey and bring pleasure and inspiration to many English readers as well.

Michelle Bromley 2025

FOREWORD TO THE ENGLISH EDITION

In the annals of Western Zen literature, few works possess quite the ability to transcend time and resonate across generations. Platov, born in 1904 in Berlin studied and practised Yoga, Physics, Medicine, Complimentary Medicine, Analytical Psychology, (Jungian Psychology) as well as Theology, and Zen Buddhism at the highest level (the latter under two of the most well-known teachers of the time in New York, and later in Kyoto Japan). He practised medicine, and worked as a Jungian analyst before giving them all up to devote his energies to the study and practice of Zen Buddhism and later to teach. It is from this rich resource in the latter part of his life that that his commentary on *The Hermit and other Zen Stories* based on *The Tales of Tokuzan* by W. J. Gabb came to exist.

Now at last this hidden gem, hidden from all those who cannot read German, is available to the English-speaking world.

The intersection of Body and Mind, and the search for human meaning, which absorbed Platov's interests from a 15-year-old schoolboy and for so many decades through his exploration of science, medicine, psychology and religion found their true home, fruition, and resting place in Rinzai Zen.

The central Zen story 'The Hermit' deserves to be read and reread, and is a masterpiece of religious writing both moving, as well as encapsulating the essence of religious life.

The quest for deeper understanding of our human condition resonates throughout the text and it is good to see that this superb translation, by Michelle Bromley, retains the German philosophical terms as well as the English approximations.

Poetry can sometimes transcend the barrier between mind and heart and this book, although not poetry, is moving at a profound level, and here it is, an oversight corrected, at last, and a gift to all those who pick up and read these pages.

Desmond Biddulph
President, The Buddhist Society
London, 2025

Dr. Henry B. Platov (doctor of medicine and theology) was born in Berlin on November 17th 1904. He studied physics and philosophy at the Alexander Humboldt Akademie in Berlin as well as medicine at the University of Berlin. During this time he also became interested in analytical psychology and for a while studied with the well-known Dr. Hans Blüher. He was also a member of the Berlin Society for Esoteric Studies and the Research Society for Parapsychology, the latter under the direction of Prof. Dr. Hans Driesch.

After completing his medical studies, H. Platov spent his time living between Berlin and New York, but in 1935 he moved to America permanently. He practised medicine and analytical psychology in New York and Florida and augmented his training with the study of eclectic medicine at the McCormick Medical College in Chicago and at the School of Naturopathy in New York. He received his American Doctoral degree (MD) in Chicago. He also attended the seminars that Dr. Carl Gustave Jung held for doctors and therapists in New York. There followed a year in London at the Intercollegiate College, Order of Antioch (today a part of London University under the name Christus Rex College) where he received a doctorate in theology (DD). A while later he was ordained as archimandrite (archpriest) of the Greek-orthodox Catholic Church.

Henry Platov's interest in Eastern philosophy began at the age of 15 when he studied Raja Yoga and was a student of Gustav Meyrink. At that time he also made the acquaintance of Prof. C. Hsu, sinologist at the Berlin University, with whom he studied about the theory and practice of early Taoism.

In 1932 H. Platov met the Japanese Zen Master Shigetsu Sasaki, known as Sokei-an in New York. Sokei-an was the first Rinzai Zen master who lived and taught in the West, though he did so from a small apartment in Manhattan. Platov practised Zen under the guidance of Sokei-an until the latter's early death in 1945. Several years later he travelled to Kyoto to study with Sokei-an's Dharma-brother, Zuigan Goto Roshi, and once again underwent a long and hard training. Goto Roshi was chief abbot of Daitoku-ji and Myoshin-ji temples, both important temples of the Rinzai tradition. In 1961 after he was authorised as a Zen teacher by Myoshin-ji, he gave up his psychotherapy practice and dedicated himself exclusively to the teaching of Zen. As a disciple of Sokei-an he is a Dharma-heir in the line of transmission from Kogaku Soen (Soyen Shaku 1860-1919), the Zen priest who spoke in America about Zen, Tetsuo Sokatsu (1870-1954) who revived the Zen lay movement in Japan, and Sokei-an (1828-1945), the founder of the First Zen Institute of America.

H. Platov then moved to Los Angelos, California and set up a zendo in his own home. During the following years Zen became very popular in America and many Zen masters arrived from Japan. When H. Platov for various reasons gave up his practice after 15 years, many training possibilities were available in both Rinzai and Soto Zen. This was not the case in Switzerland. Though Zen was no longer unknown there, thanks to the works of Graf F. Dürkheim and Soto Master Deshimara Roshi, there was no Rinzai Zen teacher living there.

At the invitation of one of his American students of Swiss descent, H. Platov visited Switzerland for the first time in 1969. A small group of students gathered around him and in the following years H. Platov regularly returned to Switzerland and either taught from his hotel room or from the private home of a student couple. In 1974 a small apartment was rented which served as a zendo. Through the initiative and perseverance of his students in Zürich the Rinzai Zen Society of Switzerland was established with its residence in Zürich. Since then, H. Platov spends several months each year there teaching Zen in the tradition of the Rinzai school. It is of great advantage that he not only speaks German but also knows the psyche and religious background of Westerners very well. His Zen lectures reflect this deep understanding through the numerous connections he makes between Zen and Christianity and Western psychology and philosophy, yet without mixing the one with the other. At the same time these lectures provide a deep insight into Zen's original roots in the Indo-Buddhistic tradition as well as the Chinese Taoist influences.

This volume contains a small selection from the numerous lectures (teiso) H. Platov gave for his students at the Shogen-Dojo in Zürich. The selection was made from a series of lectures that he gave from 1984 to 1985 under the heading 'Tales of Tokuzan'. The tales were taken from the book *The Goose is Out* by W. J. Gabb which was published in 1956 by The Buddhist Society in London. To avoid any misunderstanding, it should be pointed out that the Tokuzan of these stories is not the Chinese Zen Master Tokusan Senkan who lived from 780 to 861, but rather a fictional character created by W. J. Gabb. A practising Buddhist himself, Gabb relates how during a certain period in his life anecdotes and verses spontaneously surfaced in his imagination, stories which he had previously never heard of or read – they just came to him. Under the pseudonym Tokuzan he published these fragments at intervals in a Buddhist magazine which is now unknown. Later these articles were collected by The Buddhist Society and published as the above-mentioned book. These tales have a lot of similarity with traditional Zen anecdotes, especially with respect to their 'irrational' element that is so typical of Zen. H. Platov took much pleasure in these simple stories and decided to use some of them as the text for his commentaries. Thus this delightful encounter between the spiritual culture of a Western Zen master and that of a Western Zen text came about. On the occasion of H. Platov's 85th birthday, it seems that this unique jewel is worthy of being made available to a wider public. With this publication H. Platov in his very advanced years has finally given in to the wishes of his students and the publisher; previously he had never been willing to have any of his words published. According to the Zen tradition to which he has devoted himself, he solely emphasises actual Zen in daily life.

May this book find many readers and may it inspire people of different religions to search for the truth of their existence.

Zurich, May 1989
Agatha Wydler

THE HERMIT
AND OTHER ZEN TALES

with Commentaries by
HENRY B. PLATOV

There is a collection of stories entitled 'Tales of Tokuzan' from the book, *The Goose is Out*. The author is the Englishman, W. J. Gabb, who obviously had a very intuitive understanding of Zen. The first tale is called 'Zen Realisation'.

> Hsiang was a philosopher and there were also times when he thought to good purpose. On one of these latter occasions he came to visit Tokuzan and asked him, 'Would you say that you had a realisation?'
>
> 'I would,' replied Tokuzan.
>
> 'Is this humility?' enquired Hsiang.
>
> The Master made a deprecatory gesture. 'I am trying to help you,' he observed.
>
> 'Then show me your realisation,' Hsiang demanded.
>
> 'Show me your eyes and I will show you my realisation,' was Tokuzan's reply.
>
> Hsiang considered for a while. Then he said, 'There was a time when I, too, thought I had realisation. Now I know it was not true.'
>
> Tokuzan agreed. 'There will be a time when I shall realise my realisation is no realisation, and that will be realisation indeed. Meanwhile, I realise.'
>
> Hsiang persisted, 'How do you know that what you realise is true? A man can imagine food and wine although in fact he starves.'
>
> Tokuzan told him, 'How does a man know what he eats is true? What does a man care that what he eats is true? The food is there, he eats and is sustained. Without it he would be hungry and his work would not be done. All men know this

and no man doubts. It is even so with Suchness. I see it and I assimilate it; it nourishes me and that would seem to be well. I see others without it and I perceive they suffer from their lack. Therefore, I do not question its truth; I eat my fill. Is this unreasonable?'

'What shall I do?' enquired Hsiang.

'If you cannot eat it, sleep on it,' said the Master. After all, it was good advice.

On the one hand this story is rather amusing, on the other it is typically Zen-ish. How is one to understand what is said here? Are grand intellectual reflections useful or just plain common sense? Hsiang was a philosopher, and with slight sarcasm, it is mentioned that he occasionally thought to good purpose. Zen masters don't regard philosophising very highly, though within the framework of Buddhism one can take the liberty of philosophising. But in Zen one distinguishes between reality and thoughts about reality. Thoughts about reality nourish us as little as thoughts about soup nourish us. Only the soup itself nourishes. Thoughts about reality and reality itself are therefore two different things.

On one of the occasions where the philosopher actually 'thought to good purpose', he visited Tokuzan and asked, 'Would you say that you had a realisation?' – There are a number of stories where a philosopher, that is a serious thinker, goes to a Zen master or a Taoist master and asks questions. The answers are often quite peculiar. A well-known example for this is the story of a Zen master who sits at a little table in the garden on which a teapot and a waterpot are placed. A philosopher arrives and standing in front of the master asks, 'What is the true Way?' The master doesn't say anything, but just points up at the sky with one hand and with the other at the table. The philosopher says, 'I don't understand.' Thereupon the master says,

'The cloud in the sky, the water in the pot.' He doesn't say that the true Way is Buddhism, Zen, or any other philosophy or worldview. He simply states, 'The cloud in the sky, the water in the pot.' That is the true Way. Nothing more! Nowadays this answer is used as a koan and the student has to try and understand it without any help.

When Hsiang asked the master whether it was humility to claim to have had a realisation, the master made a deprecatory gesture and said, 'I'm trying to help you.' Thereupon Hsiang demanded, 'If you have a realisation, then show it.' – Don't just natter on, show me this realisation! One has to admit, that is pretty good for a philosopher. The man wasn't as rigidly intellectual as many of his fellow philosophers. That is why it is said that there were times when he also thought to good purpose and didn't just idly philosophise. Thereupon Tokuzan replied, 'Show me your eyes and I will show you my realisation.' – What does that mean? What does one do with the eyes? One sees. What does one see? Whatever comes before one's eyes. With what do the eyes see?

Three factors always need to be present for perception and awareness to take place: first of all the sense organ, secondly that which acts on the sense organ, and thirdly consciousness. If one of these three is missing, then there is nothing to see, hear, etc. That is a fact. If I close the eyes, the object is not there and there is nothing to see. I can, however, have a picture of this object, but then the question arises whether the picture I have in my consciousness is objective or subjective. This, too, is a question that Zen concerns itself with. If the eye is there and open, but there is no object, then there is nothing to see either. And if there is an eye and an object, but no consciousness, then likewise there is nothing to see. All three factors belong together, they so to speak constitute a unity. Naturally impressions made on the sense organs will also influence consciousness. That begins as soon as life emerges. That is why Tokuzan says, 'Show me your eyes and I will show you my realisation.'

Hsiang considered this for a while and then said, 'There was a time when I, too, thought I had a realisation. Now I know it was not true.' – One has certain notions and assumptions, based either on thinking or perceiving or feeling, and these are our reality. One imagines or presumes one has had a realisation. Then one discovers that one didn't have one. A philosopher might think he has realised something, then he is confronted by a person like Tokuzan and suddenly discovers that he hasn't had a realisation after all.

Tokuzan agreed, 'There will be a time when I shall realise my realisation is no realisation, and that will be realisation indeed. Meanwhile, I realise.' – That is actually a very normal process. At first one thinks one has realised something, then one sees that one hasn't had a realisation, which of course is a realisation. To realise that one hasn't realised is a realisation. This repeats itself and takes its course so that in the time between realising and realising non-realisation, one realises. This process is very interesting and one should become aware of it and understand it. What is it that actually sees, realises or thinks it is realising and then says, 'I thought I had a realisation, but it isn't a realisation after all.'

Now Hsiang continues, 'How do you know that what you realise is true? A man can imagine food and wine although in fact he starves.' – As I already mentioned, it is very important in Zen to distinguish between words and thoughts about a thing and the actual thing itself. For instance, one can imagine how nice and warm the sunshine is, but if one doesn't leave the dark cold room, one remains pale and feels cold. However, as soon as one goes out into the sun, one feels warm and gets a tan. So Tokuzan replies, 'How does a man know what he eats is true? What does a man care that what he eats is true? The food is there, he eats and is sustained. Without it he would be hungry and his work would not be done. All men know this and no man doubts.'

– But we should bear in mind that everything in this existence is a process of actualisation, that out of the non-visible the visible comes forth like the oak from the acorn or matter from energy frequencies or deeds from ideas, from good ideas as well as from bad ideas. The nourishment is there, and we eat it. Tokuzan is very realistic and also typically Chinese. The Chinese always think about the stomach first. When two Chinese people meet, they ask one another, 'How is your stomach, how are your bones?', just as we say, 'How are you? How's it going?' Then Tokuzan added, 'It is even so with Suchness.' – That is the salient point of this story. The Sanskrit word for 'Suchness' is *bhutatathata*. One should see things in their Suchness. That is firmly emphasised in Zen. It is an expression of profound actuality. In the *Tao-te-ching* Lao-tzu says that with the constantly desiring spirit one only sees the outer shell of things, that is, their appearance; but with the spirit free of desire, one sees the essence of things, one sees things in their Suchness. What kind of things? In Chinese or Taoist texts, the 'ten thousand things' are frequently referred to. It means 'all things' inclusive of sentient things – living beings – and the so-called non-sentient things. Human beings are also things, composed of many things. The body is a thing, the sense organs are things through which one perceives all kinds of things, and then there are things that are thought, things felt, etc. We live in a world of things. Expressed in terms of epistemology it is a phenomenal world. It is the world as it appears to us. We don't see the world in its Suchness. From a psychological point of view, we humans see what we project onto things and think we are seeing reality. This self-deception is not only recognised by psychologists, but is also backed up by the natural sciences. It is worthwhile looking more closely into this strange mechanism that only allows us to see the surface of things, but not their essence. Let's take an ordinary object, for example, this small zendo singing bowl. A person sees this object for the first time and doesn't know what it is. Perhaps they think it's an ashtray, for there isn't any elsewhere in the room. Or they might think it's a water or tea bowl. Perhaps they have no thoughts about it. Another person ascertains that the object is made of metal and feels cool to the touch. Then they discover that it produces a sound when struck. Eventually one finds out that it is neither an ashtray nor a spittoon, but a sounding box. It was made to produce a specific sound. Do you like the sound? 'No, I don't like it, the tone is too thin. I want a deeper tone.' Is it a thin sound? Is it an unpleasant tone? It is not the ear that judges, nor is it the object. The judgement lies with us. There is something amiss with our consciousness and consequently we see the bowl only as an object and hear its sound only with regard to our likes or dislikes.

That is only a small example, a small matter. I could, of course, also cite examples that mean more to us than this little object here: a flower, a small or large animal or a human being. These are all compounded things, regardless of whether they are large or small. With the desiring spirit one only sees their shell, the exterior layer. But with the spirit free of desire, one sees the essence of things. One sees things in their Suchness. The famous poet, Gertrude Stein, wrote, 'A rose is a rose, is a rose.'

The realisation of Suchness is what is important in Zen. My teacher, Sokei-an, coined the expression 'is-ness' for this. Just as it is. The bird in the tree who builds its nest and chirps, knows of the is-ness of the tree. But a human standing in front of the tree hasn't got the faintest idea about it. He stands there completely baffled. Naturally he can say it's a fir tree or a fruit tree, that he can do. But for the bird the tree simply is what it is. It doesn't know it in the sense that a human does, but for it the tree exists in its Suchness. Humans, however, have the possibility of realising Suchness, the essence of all things. Hence the Buddha said, that though we humans have gone astray and suffer, we should nonetheless consider ourselves fortunate to be born as humans, for we have the possibility of coming to the realisation of ourselves.

Humans pollute their environment, but not just the outside environment as ecology shows us, but also the inside one. With the help of psychology we then try to put the spoiled inside back in order again. Ecology tries to see things in their Suchness, their connectedness, in their own existence. How does it stand with human society in its Suchness? We know that it is in a sorry state, we more or less know how it's not working well. But we need to have a knowledge of Suchness. The bird doesn't need this knowledge, it lives out of it. But people should try and attain this knowledge.

Tokuzan said, 'I see it (Suchness) and assimilate it; it nourishes me and that would seem to be well.' This expression 'it seems to be well' is again very typically Chinese. The Chinese people, but also the Japanese, are always very careful. For instance, Chuang-tzu said, 'It seems as though people have a soul, for if they didn't have a soul they would have no visibility.' He didn't say, 'They *have* a soul', he said, 'It seems as though.'

When one is in a Japanese Zen temple and observes the monks, one notices how they accept things, including themselves, in their Suchness. If one accepts oneself in Suchness, then it is *that* (*tathata*). But if one doesn't see oneself in Suchness, but only as that which one projects onto oneself and says, 'This is me', then there are difficulties. Have you ever asked yourselves what kind of self-portrait you have of yourselves, how you see yourselves – mentally and emotionally? Do you see yourself there in your Suchness? No, you always see yourselves on the basis of self-deceptions. In the Sanskrit tradition this expression reads, '*Tat tvam asi*' – which in English means 'That you are'. You are neither this nor that, or whatever you imagine yourself to be. To recognise self-deception and accept Suchness is a process of assimilation. It is ingestion, digestion and defecation, just like with the intake of nourishment. Defecation doesn't just take place on the toilet, there is also a mental and spiritual elimination.

Finally, Hsiang asks what he should do, to which Tokuzan answers, 'If you can't eat it, sleep on it.' In any case, that was good advice. – But what does it mean, 'Sleep on it.' All forms of existence (Dasein) in the world of phenomena exist in something essential – in being (Sein). In philosophical terms it is expressed as: existence exists in Being. Or one speaks of being and becoming. In the *Tao-te-ching* it says, 'The ten thousand things emerge from Being, but Being comes from Non-being.' When one sleeps, in the natural deep sleep, one is in a state of Non-being, even though one is physically present. It is a state of being in Non-being. One exists – but there is something that sleeps – a person, a cat, a dog. But they are gone. It is an actual state of Non-being. One re-emerges from this state and appears amidst everything one is surrounded by. If one wants to express it psychologically, one would have to say: There is consciousness, and sometimes consciousness is gone. The absence of consciousness is called the unconscious. Out of it, consciousness again arises. There is consciousness in the unconscious – when one is conscious – and there is the unconscious in consciousness, because the unconscious never leaves, it is always there. This is not just dialectics, it is reality. That is why Tokuzan said, 'If you can't eat it, sleep on it.'

The next story of Tokuzan is called 'Zen Belief'. Zen is a school within Buddhism, and Buddhism is a religion. It is usually said that religions are a matter of belief. Every religion is a matter of belief. Whether one believes in God, as the Christian religion does, or in a supernatural power as other religions do, or whether one has any other conception of the divine – it is all a matter of belief. However, belief should not be blind faith, as was clearly stated by St. Paul, who said belief must be based on understanding.

Buddhism has never recognised a God or any intellectually created omnipotent beings. Buddhism is a very philosophical religion, deeply contemplated, and carefully analysed down to the finest points. In this respect one could say that Buddhism is not a matter of belief. First and foremost, it is a religion of realisation, not of belief. The emphasis is on enlightenment, whereas in Christianity the emphasis is on belief. Admittedly Jesus did speak of the knowledge of truth that liberates. On the other hand, he said to a healed man, 'Your faith has healed you.' So, Buddhism is a religion of knowing, a quasi-gnostic religion. Nonetheless, the title of this story is 'Zen Belief'.

There is a very famous koan that deals with the question of belief in Zen. It goes back to Eno (Hui-neng), the Sixth Patriarch of Zen in China. He is regarded as the greatest patriarch and the actual founder of Zen. He emphasised sudden enlightenment as opposed to gradual enlightenment. After the Fifth Patriarch had appointed Eno as successor, he advised him to leave the temple as the monks would be angry with him, because they were expecting another monk, the eldest among them, to be designated as the Sixth Patriarch. The old master feared the monks would kill his successor, so he sent him away. Eno did as he was told, but a few monks pursued him. Again and again, he was able to elude his pursuers by hiding and covering his tracks. This went on for a long time, until Eno grew weary of this pursuit. One day he hid behind a large rock, until the pursuing monks were close by. Then he stood up and showed himself completely. His pursuers were naturally surprised and stood still. Eno laid his robe and begging bowl on the rock in front of him and very calmly said, 'This robe and begging bowl are the symbol of my belief. Take the robe and bowl with you, and I will resign as successor of the Fifth Patriarch.' The leader of the monks wanted to take the robe and bowl from the stone, but could not. The robe and bowl, the symbol of Eno's belief, could not be taken away. The corresponding koan reads: What is belief?

What in fact is belief? Normally one says I believe *in* something, I believe *in* God, or I believe *in* a supernatural power. A child believes in its father and mother, we believe in the sincerity of others, in love, etc. This belief should, of course, not disappoint, and when it does, it leads to sadness. We might believe in Almighty God, but then this or that misfortune occurs and we ask, 'Why did God allow that to happen? Why does this happen to me and not to someone else, why me of all people?' Children are also disappointed by their parents. Sometimes parents casually make promises and the child is disappointed when its expectations are not fulfilled. Then doubts arise, doubts on what is believed in and doubt on belief itself. In Zen doubt is taken very seriously, because it is only through doubt that one can arrive at certainty. That is very paradoxical: on the one hand belief, on the other doubt. But belief should not be blind faith, belief should be based on understanding. And that is why doubt is emphasised in Zen. One doubts everything imaginable until one arrives at the Great Doubt. The first doubts concern small matters, but then the big doubt comes and from this doubt true belief emerges. Listen now to the story about Tokuzan:

A monk came to Tokuzan seeking enlightenment. He had been studying under the Master Huang Tzu for years without result. He thought the teaching was at fault; therefore he sought elsewhere. All this he explained at the initial interview.

Tokuzan said, 'There is only one teaching in Zen Buddhism. What did Huang Tzu teach?'

The monk replied, 'He told me to believe in everything. In going and coming, in boiled rice and in the day before yesterday. In fact, in everything.'

The Master commented, 'Belief in everything includes belief in the unreal. What of the horns of a hair?'

'In such I have not believed,' the monk admitted.

Tokuzan dismissed him. He said, 'The path calls for patience and persistence. It also entails pursuance to the end. When you believe a hare has horns, we may progress.'

The monk retired to meditate. He finally managed to persuade himself that a hare indeed has horns. He communicated this to the Master.

'So far, so good,' he was told. 'And now, can you believe in nothing?'

The monk confessed his inability. Tokuzan said, 'Belief in everything includes belief in nothing. When you believe in nothing, let me know.'

The monk meditated afresh. He pondered night and day. Weeks passed and again he presented himself. He said, 'Master, I am afraid. I now believe in nothing, save this only, that I shall soon go mad.'

Tokuzan regarded him attentively. He then enquired, 'Has it occurred to you to believe in the utter, abysmal absurdity of expecting to attain the unthinkable by any process of thought whatsoever?'

The monk shook his head. This thought had not occurred to him. He paled in his despair.

In the pre-Buddhist, Indian schools in which *atman* – the true self – is emphasised it is said that nothing whatsoever can be revealed. Whenever one says or thinks *atman*, one has to say '*neti, neti*' at the same time. That means, 'not this, not that'. When one thinks that *atman* is this or that, it is not so – *neti, neti*. It is exactly the same here: 'it is an abysmal absurdity to believe one can attain the unthinkable by any process of thought whatsoever.' Even in the Jewish religion, out of which the Christian religion developed, one holds that it is impossible to conceive of an idea of God. For that reason, he is not given a name with which he could be identified. Things get an identity through names. So, God was given a name that had no meaning. The subject of the nameless God is examined in Jewish mysticism, in the Kabbalah.

So, in answer to the question of whether he had ever thought of how absurd it was to try and grasp the unthinkable by a thought process, the monk shook his head. 'This thought had not occurred to him. He paled in his despair.'

Tokuzan reassured him and said, 'A man is born a thing alive, and a thing alive must grow. But whereas in the flesh a child grows into a man, in the spirit a man grows into a child.'

This recollects the words of Jesus, 'Unless you change and become like little children, you will never enter the kingdom of heaven.' Naturally it's not a heaven you go to after you die and sit at God's feet and play a harp into all eternity or become a trumpet angel. It is a heaven in a very concrete sense. You cannot enter heaven unless you become like a small child. Even depth psychology refers to the small child, the *puer aeternus*, as the psyche inherent in the eternal child. The alchemists know the *mysterium*, that is born out of the spirit of the *homunculus*. It is interesting how the symbolism of the child as the unadulterated human being manifests itself everywhere in one form or another. There must be some truth that underlies this. It doesn't matter whether this symbolism is expressed in the framework of Buddhism, Hinduism or a Western religion, it doesn't matter if it's about Indians, Asians or Europeans or about the culture of today or tomorrow – that is of no significance. This is a question of fundamental reality. So, Tokuzan pointed out that whereas the body of a youth grows into a man, the spirit of a man develops into a child. But what is meant by this child is not the childish person that is lodged in all of us and creates difficulties for us. It is the original child. This little child is still very close to the original being (Urwesen) in the sense of Mahayana Buddhism. Later this is no longer the case. Then all kinds of conditions become established out of which the later child develops with all its difficulties, which are carried on into adulthood. This later child is shaped by its parents and the environment, whereas the early child is not yet moulded by the circumstances of life.

Tokusan continued and explained a little more what the little child is all about, saying,

'Let nature now supply your need.'

The young child still lives in close touch with nature. That I-centeredness that appears later isn't there yet. There is still a being-at-one with everything around. When it plays in the sandbox something wonderful can emerge from its nature – a castle, mountains, valleys, an entire world, all out of this simple material. It still possesses a power of imagination that is not bound by anything.

The return to this child is naturally a matter of consciousness, that is, one has to become aware of this child within oneself. But if one is only preoccupied with oneself, wrapped up in one's own thoughts and feelings or with what others think of one, then one can't reflect on this inner original being. Tokuzan carried on,

> 'Let hills offer you the breast. Let grasses whisper confidences and let trees be your tutors. Live alone in woods and fields and then come back and say.'

That is exactly what the Brahmins did. They resided in the forests and composed the great teaching of the *Upanishads* – the very highest realisation of the *Vedas*.

> The monk did as directed. He returned to the womb from which he came and thence was born anew.

When Nicodemus asked Jesus how he could come to the Truth, Jesus replied, 'You have to be born again.' To which Nicodemus replied,' How can I return to the womb of my mother?' Jesus answered, 'You call yourself Israel's teacher and do not understand these words? You have to be born again of water and spirit.' In Buddhism it is said, you have to be reborn of water and fire.

So the monk returned to the womb from which he came. In Christian mysticism this would be understood as returning to the womb of God, becoming one with God. In the Indian religion it is expressed as Atman is Brahman and Brahman is Atman. In Zen Buddhism the same thing is expressed as, 'The dewdrop slips into the shining sea.' These are all metaphorical expressions of an actual experience. In Taoism one is encouraged to 'return to the root and nourish it.' And the word 'religion', too, as a derivation of 'religare' points to the same thing. In the truest sense of the word, religion is a re-linking, being 're-delivered' (Zurückentbindung) back into the womb of the origin. In Zen koan training, the emphasis is placed on the realisation of the dharmakaya. The *dharmakaya* is the ground from which everything originates. It is the womb of being and becoming. It is out of this womb that the monk was reborn.

The story continues,

> Thereafter he drank his fill at the fount of life and grew steadily in the Tao.

Bodhidharma brought the Buddhist Meditation School (*dhyana*) from India to China. There it was called '*ch'an-na*' or '*ch'an*', which became 'Zen' in Japan. But even before Bodhidharma came to China, a form of meditation already existed there, as well as the concept of the Tao. Both were integrated into Zen. The Sanskrit word '*dharma*' was replaced by '*Tao*' and are therefore interchangeable in Zen. So, when it says that the monk grew steadily in the Tao, it means that his understanding of the Dharma grew.

> He found that a man who is deaf to his fellowman may have ears for the grasses and trees.

What does that mean to be deaf to one's fellowmen? Especially nowadays we are always being told how important it is to communicate with one another; not to be withdrawn, but to come out of ourselves and cultivate social activities. Zen is really such a tricky business, it is contrary to everything one is used to doing…but deaf to one's fellowmen means that one shouldn't listen to the gossip of others, and naturally also not to one's own all too human nonsense with which one mentally entertains oneself and identifies with. In this kind of exchange, we only offload our own psychic contents on others. That should cease. The monk noticed that when he was deaf to the constant chatter of his fellowmen, he had ears for the grasses and trees.

The text goes on to say,

> They told him much in the early days but soon he was telling them more. After all, it was inevitable, for grass and trees are grass and trees...

They exist in their Suchness, they are simply grasses and trees, natural and perfect in their total essence, not just on the surface.

> ... but man is revealed as man.

In the human being, what is truly human is revealed. That which isn't human is the mineral world, the plant world and the animal world. These worlds are present in our human cells as memories or inheritance and are thus actually manifested. Usually, however, we are not aware of them, we do not penetrate these worlds, we are too preoccupied with what is going on in and around us. In order to really penetrate through to this true nature, we have to stop all our inner and outer chatter. The mineral world is present in our bones, the plant world is contained, for example, in our autonomous nervous system and the animal world in our perceptions and feelings. In order to reveal what is truly human, one must penetrate into all these worlds. What does it mean that the monk soon told the grasses and trees more than they told him. In Mahayana Buddhism there is the Bodhisattva ideal. A Bodhisattva is someone, who having attained realisation does not then dwell on the highest mountain peaks, but returns to the valleys to help people follow the way that helped him. He vows to assist all the innumerable beings to attain realisation. These innumerable beings exist within ourselves: the grasses and trees and animals and beings that live in and around us. That which is truly human, namely realisation, should be brought into all these realms. How does one do this? One practises meditation, for example. Everything that is described in this story is a method of meditation. In the Indian tradition there is a form of meditation in which one becomes one with the tree or stone in front of one. This oneness is called *samjana*. Through this unification one realises the essence of all things. One doesn't grapple with them or run away from them. Quite the contrary. That is why the text says that 'man is revealed as man' and perceptual awareness (*manas*) addresses the grasses and trees and tells them more then they tell him.

And so it was that belief grew to knowledge,

This sentence can be understood as the koan, 'What is belief?' that I mentioned at the beginning.

and knowledge grew in turn to a simple awareness.

Awareness – the key word of Zen. What is one aware of? One can stare at the tip of one's nose until one goes cross-eyed and then one has an awareness focussed on oneself. The inner eyes of humans are usually concentrated on their own nose. In yoga there is a breathing exercise – *pranayama* – in which one actually directs the awareness to the tip of the nose, and mentally observes the in- and out-breath. But that is something else. The ordinary self-centeredness of human beings is not a simple awareness. But the text describes this simple awareness as that

of which a man who is capable of simple awareness is simply aware.

And only humans can do this.

> In time, simplicity achieved, he sought out Tokuzan. The
> Master rose to meet him. 'Tell me,' he demanded. 'What
> have you attained?' The monk regarded him ruefully. 'I
> have gathered a million mosquito bites.' Tokuzan sat down
> satisfied. He called for tea and salve.

When someone says that they want to attain enlightenment and envisions this or that outcome – like a higher consciousness or something like that – then their expectations are already completely fixed. For that reason, there is also the famous story about the master who sees one of his monks sitting in the garden meditating and asks what he is doing. The monk answers, 'I am meditating.' To which the master asks, 'To what purpose?' 'To become a Buddha,' the monk answered. Thereupon the master said, 'That's a great idea, I think I'll join you.' He sat down next to the monk, picked up a nearby stone and began rubbing it with the sleeve of his robe. The monk's curiosity got the better of him and he asked the master what he was doing. 'I'm polishing a stone,' replied the master. 'To what end?' asked the monk. 'I want to make it into a mirror,' replied the master. The student asked 'How can polishing a stone make it into a mirror?' Whereupon the master asked, 'How can meditating make a Buddha?' The same matter is addressed here when Tokuzan asks, 'What have you attained?' The monk regarded Tokuzan ruefully – of course, we do not know whether this was an expression of feigned self-pity or if the monk felt sorry for Tokuzan. But in a way it is the same thing, because monk and master mirrored one another. In Zen this is called 'mingling eyebrows', or we would say seeing eye to eye. The monk naturally wasn't fooled by the master's question, and didn't say, 'I have attained simple awareness.' or 'I came to this or that realisation.' He just said, 'I have gathered a million mosquito bites,' after all, he had been spending some time in the forest. The master sat down satisfied. The fact that he stood up to greet his pupil is an indication that he knew immediately what the monk had achieved as soon as he entered. Now he called for tea and salve.

THE HERMIT

Tokuzan was walking through the market of a near-by town. He noticed, in particular, a vendor of millet-seed vociferously shouting the virtues of his commodity. Finally, he entered into conversation with the man, and was surprised by his wise remarks.

'For a vendor of millet-seeds you make an admirable philosopher,' he observed.

'As a hermit I have plenty of time for meditation,' the man agreed.

'Did you say hermit?' asked the Master, thinking he had misheard.

The man waved his hand to indicate the jostling crowd and recited:

> Owing to the exigencies of circumstance,
> My last remnants of privacy have been removed.
> Now, my seclusion is complete.

'Remarkable,' said Tokuzan. 'Will you please explain?'

The man continued, 'Long time since, I wished to retire from the world and become a hermit. However, I was smitten with the love-sickness and took a wife instead. She bore me many children, including several fine but noisy sons. Still, I longed for the seclusion in which to meditate, but the demands my family made upon me increased, and my leisure hours became less and less. Finally, when all my time was occupied, I went away, and now I live alone in the bosom of my family and the clamour of the market. I doubt if I shall come back.' He proffered a handful of millet-seeds.

Tokuzan marvelled as he accepted the seeds. 'In the whole

of China, I should say you have no equal.'

Good-humouredly, the man remonstrated, 'In the whole of China there is none else but I.'

This is a good story. It runs quite contrary to the usual ideas we have about hermits. How can the man claim to be a hermit and have lots of time for meditation, when he finds himself in the bosom of his family and in the hustle and bustle of the market place? Doesn't a hermit withdraw from the world, from all distractions and demands, and meditate in order to penetrate within and find himself? In any case, that's the usual view. You can read everywhere that in order to meditate and find the stillness within, you need to find a quiet place. Whether it concerns the meditation of a Christian mystic, of a Sufi, an Indian yogi or a Zen student, the advice is always, 'Find a quiet spot, retire there and find the stillness within yourself.'

My teacher, Sokei-an, used to say, 'It's no big feat to sit in a zendo and meditate. But what about here in New York City on the corner of 42th Street and Broadway? This is probably the busiest corner in the whole world; it's hard to imagine the noisy traffic and the teeming crowds, where every social stratum of humanity can be found, from builders and bankers, beggars and pimps, to shoppers and drifters. You should place yourselves on this corner and meditate. If you can maintain a state of meditation in this throng, then your meditation is really good.'

In the Zen tradition you are expected to try and take your seat of meditation with you into all your activities. This of course doesn't mean your sitting cushion, but your inner seat, *hara*. After you have done zazen, get up and attend to your daily duties, but bring your inner seat into all your activities and your comings and goings. Never leave your seat of meditation whether you are thinking, feeling, hearing or seeing. If one is able to do this, then the state of meditation is carried over into all activities, and then everything one does becomes a meditation. By becoming one with everything one does, one forgets oneself completely. The state of meditation is not something one creates, it is a state that already exists as such and that one becomes aware of through concentration. One enters this existing state and becomes one with it. This becoming one with often occurs automatically, without our realising it. If, for example, one is engrossed in reading a book, one forgets oneself completely. Or at the cinema, one can become one with the events playing out on the screen. However, in this case we are not conscious of this state, whereas in meditation we are aware of it. We should become rooted in it like a seed in the earth. One has to develop the strength to remain in this state. That is the purpose of zazen, of sitting meditation. As long as the seed doesn't yet have roots, it can easily be washed away by rain. But as soon as its roots have formed and sunk deeper into the soil, it can no longer be easily swept away by wind and rain. It is the same with zazen. One sits in order to become rooted in the very deepest ground of consciousness. Then one is no longer carried away by circumstances. Whatever approaches us from the outside or what happens on the inside, it will not carry us away.

The millet-vender said, 'Owing to the exigencies of circumstance, my last remnants of privacy have been removed. Now, my seclusion is complete.' – How should that be understood? As an I-conscious being we are preoccupied with ourselves, with our private person, our thoughts, feelings, words and deeds. We say 'my' thoughts, 'my' feelings, 'my' reactions, 'my' experience, etc. Personal identity and the concomitant self-preoccupation determine everything. Yet in meditation we are asked to get away from ourselves. The 'I' should step aside, and one should enter into that which is 'No-I'. We should also not take the I into other worlds. There are forms of meditation, where one takes the I into other realms of consciousness, just like ones interesting dreams, but that is not what is meant here. The millet-vender got away from his 'I' thanks to the demands of his circumstances. But his going away must be understood correctly. One leaves behind the preoccupation with oneself and all the stuff that is associated with it. For a long time he wanted to retire from the world. As this concerns a Zen story, it means that he wanted to go into a monastery or a remote hermit's hut. But instead he got married, had many children and got more and more wrapped up in duties. And so he could no longer attend to himself. He didn't have any leisure hours to withdraw into a room in his house to meditate.

'Now I live alone in the bosom of my family and the clamour of the market. I doubt if I shall ever come back,' – that is to say, if I will ever return to a private life. Through meditation one arrives at a state called *samadhi*, where I-consciousness disappears. But pure consciousness, absolute awareness remains. In the famous story of *Alice in Wonderland* there is the description of the Cheshire Cat, who sits on a branch and grins. Then the cat gradually disappears and only the grin remains. The English writer R. H. Blyth, who lived in Japan for many years and also translated haiku, wrote a book about Zen in English literature. There he mentions the grin of the Cheshire Cat that remains long after the cat has disappeared. We have the same thing in this story: the private person is gone. A very famous teacher, Aleister Crowley, was once asked to define yoga. Not wasting any words, he simply said, 'Sit down, shut up and get out.' Go away, clear off! – 'Finally, when all my time was occupied, I went away, and now I live alone in the bosom of my family.' *Alone*! 'Tokuzan marvelled, "In all of China I should say you have no equal." Good-humouredly, the man remonstrated, "In the whole of China there is none else but I."'

What is the meaning of this, 'none else but I'? Legend has it that after the Buddha was born from the armpit of his mother, he immediately stood up and with one hand pointing to heaven and the other to the earth said, 'In the whole world, I alone am the World-honoured One.' That is the same as the millet-vender saying, 'There is none else but I.' We are all one. We are of one essence, in a state of primordial being (Urwesen). But if one adamantly only focusses on one's own individuality, one can't say that. Every human being is really *atman*, the true self, and *atman* is one with *brahman*. That is how it is expressed in Indian religion. In the Christian religion it is said that human beings are created in the image and likeness of God, that means out of the same essence as God. Viewed in this light, there are not thousands upon thousands of different people, but, in the truest sense of the word, only one person. When one has divested oneself of all apparel and coverings, one becomes aware of this sameness. The Indian expression for this is *Tat tvam asi* – That you are. Everyone is exactly the same. We are of one and the same essence. That is not something imagined or a theoretical assumption. That is simply how it is.

In the olden days, when someone wanted to enter a Zen monastery, they would be asked what they wanted here. If they should say, 'I want to attain enlightenment,' the answer would be, 'There's nothing like that here, but you can come in and help clean, cook rice and make the tea.' Through giving oneself wholly into these activities, what is small, the private person, recedes ever more, until it finally disappears altogether. Then the great becomes apparent and reveals the unity. This isn't just the case in Zen monasteries or in an Indian ashram, the same thing occurs in the army. In the army the individual steps back and becomes a component of the army. Each component of this army is important, not as an individual, but as a part of the whole. My teacher experienced this too. He was enlisted during the Russo-Japanese War and had to serve as a soldier in the army, even though he was a monk. His individuality didn't count, he had to be a soldier. But even during this time as a soldier he didn't leave his seat of meditation.

It might be difficult for you as private individuals to understand what is being discussed in this story: to be a hermit in the midst of all the activities, in all the circumstances that unfold outside and inside ourselves. In meditation, inside and outside or spirit and matter, however you want to call it, become one. This is how the final words of the millet-vender are to be understood: 'In the whole of China there is none else but I.' Everyone should realise that they are a hermit.

Sokei-an lived and taught in a small one-room flat on a busy street in New York City. He referred to this living space as his hermitage. He was a hermit. He had long ago bid farewell to his private person. Those who practise zazen know how difficult it is to get away from oneself. But if one then thinks that one might as well just throw oneself into life, one soon discovers that it is just as difficult to get away from oneself there.

I often hear you say, that as an individual one should try and do justice to one's 'own' nature. But whose nature is this 'own' nature? Somehow one has to try and get away from this I-orientation, in order to find the One that is the same in everything, the common denominator. One has to go away and not come back. One has to say farewell to this erroneous self in order to recognise *Tat tvam asi* – that you are, a hermit in this existence. Each of us is that, everyone!

SATORI

The title of the next story of Tokuzan is 'Satori'. Satori is the Japanese word for enlightenment. There are a great many ideas about what satori is, and much has already been said and written about it. But that, of course, is not satori, just words about satori. One can also say any number of things about love, but that doesn't come anywhere near actual love.

Ki Lou was a kitchen monk. His labour was menial and monotonous, his meditations were long since barren of result. Crossing the courtyard on his way to work, he felt so great a need for consolation that he called silently on his mother for aid. Now his mother had been dead some years, but it was mothering that he craved and hence his voiceless call.

Immediately, it seemed to him, a great light shone on his right, and for a timeless moment an indefinable presence brought comfort and assurance. He walked hardly seeing, and when he reached the kitchen, he burst into alternate laughing and weeping.

He thought, 'I have known Satori,' and could hardly contain himself until he recounted the experience to Tokuzan.

The Master heard him to the end and then answered him kindly. 'The Satori that can be known as Satori is no Satori. Sweet music, too, can bring a man to tears. True Satori is devoid of emotion, and of intellectual comment. Show me now your hands.'

The monk spread out his fingers. 'Do you see Satori in your hands?' The monk gazed intently, but he saw nothing but flesh and felt nothing but mystification.

'Look into and through them, see them in time and space,

yet existing out of time and space. See them as serviceable implements, as a razor or a chopper. Use them in acts of service and deeds of love. No use to look elsewhere for your Satori. When you once know Satori, you can see it anywhere at any time. It is ever present and ever to be experienced by a simple focusing of the attention; it is known as you know yourself.'

Ki Lou returned to his kitchen with new courage and a new dignity. For when a man is aware that his past, his present and his future lie in his own hands, then, though a kitchen be his Karma, he is captain of his soul.

So, 'Ki Lou was a kitchen monk. His labour was menial and monotonous, and his meditations were long since barren of result.' – This actually happens. When one lives in a monastery as a monk for a long time, there comes a point when one doesn't seem to make any headway, a state like stagnant water. As long as one is struggling to pass the barrier of a koan, which can sometimes make one angry or depressed, something is still happening, something is going on. But after this intensive phase, one arrives at a state where nothing is happening, as if one were inwardly vegetating, but outwardly one goes about doing what has to be done – kitchen duties, cleaning, chopping wood. Ki Lou was in such a state where he seemed to be stagnating inwardly.

'Crossing the courtyard on his way to work, he felt so great a need for consolation that he called silently on his mother for aid. Now his mother had been dead some years, but it was mothering that he craved and hence his voiceless call. Immediately, it seemed to him, a great light shone on his right, and for a timeless moment an indefinable presence brought comfort and assurance. He walked hardly seeing, and when he reached the kitchen, he burst into alternate laughing and weeping.' – This description is also very true to life. It can sometimes happen that when there is such a strong outpouring of emotion, we either burst out laughing or break down into tears. Although such a reaction does have significance, I would like to point out that there is another kind of laughter, like Hotei's, the Buddha with the large belly who mingled around the villages. Because people knew he was enlightened they approached him with all kinds of questions: What is nirvana? What is the essence of the Buddhist teachings? What is rebirth all about? What does karma mean? Etc.

Such a story doesn't actually need a commentary; it speaks for itself, very simply and clearly. However, because one has such lofty ideas about enlightenment and satori, it is perhaps necessary to look at it a bit more closely. In place of satori, another term is also used, namely *kensho*. The word *kensho* is less charged with grandiose ideas than the word satori. *Kensho* simply means 'to see into one's true nature', into one's original being. When Master Tokuzan says to Ki Lou, 'Do you see satori in your hands?', he is pointing at this *kensho*. Look into your true nature, into your original being, and then see the manifestation of this true nature, this original being.

'The monk saw nothing but flesh and felt nothing but mystification.' In the *Tao-te-ching* we read: 'With a heart that is constantly desiring, one sees only the outer shell of things; with a heart that is free of desire, one sees into the innermost essence of things.' This sentence and its connotations cannot be repeated often enough. When we see something, an item, an object, it is across from us. The light-waves that alight on this object are, as it were, bounced back. We only see the surface. We don't see through the object. Neither do we see through ourselves, or through other people, and we also don't see through the so-called insentient things, because we see them all only as objects. In addition to that, our own notions come into play, that is, we don't just see the surface of things, but also that which we project onto them. We have certain ideas about ourselves and others, and according to these we perceive ourselves and engage with others. But that doesn't lead anywhere. That is why Tokuzan tells Li Kou, 'Look into and through them, see them as things in time and space, yet existing out of time and space.' – Simultaneously! When one practises meditation correctly, that is, meditation without images or themes, meditation where one doesn't entertain oneself – because there are forms of meditation which are quite entertaining, where one visualises all sorts of things, some of which are rather ridiculous, but others deeply profound – anyway, when one practises 'objectless' (vorstellungslos) meditation, then, on the one hand one sees things in time and space and on the other hand outside of time and space, and this simultaneously. How does one achieve this?

In this kind of 'objectless' meditation one abandons all things, the entire contents of consciousness and enters into a state outside of time and space. Pure consciousness, without contents and features is in itself outside of time and space. One lets go of all desires, of all attachment to things including thoughts and feelings. One lets go and enters into this consciousness outside of time and space. After a certain time, one steps out of this state in which one had relinquished everything and was immersed in emptiness, and then time and space are there again with all the form and substance that they contain. Then one becomes aware that one really sees 'things in time and space, yet existing out of time and space' and does so simultaneously. In the *Heart Sutra* (Jap. *Hannya Shingyo*) it says, 'Form is not different from no-form, and no-form is not different from form.' In Zen training this is chanted throughout the day. Yet this should not just be recited like a parrot, without thinking – one should ask oneself what is actually meant by, 'Form is not different from no-form, and no-form is not different from form.' Or as it is expressed at the very highest level of realisation, 'Samsara is nirvana, and nirvana is samsara.' That is easily said, but it's not an intellectual statement, nor a matter of feeling, and I repeat: it is by far the very highest insight. It is the first and the last, the alpha and omega.

'Look at your hands and see them as serviceable implements' – in time and space – 'as a razor or a chopper. Use them in acts of service and in deeds of love.' The emphasis on love is found not only in the Christian religion, but also in Buddhism. There this love is called *karuna*. In Hinduism it is *bhakti*. In Bhakti-yoga everything one does, is done out of love for Krishna. 'Use all things in acts of service and in deeds of love. No use to look elsewhere for your Satori.' Nowhere outside can satori be found, only within oneself. Naturally not in an egotistic self-centredness, but in the sense of embodying your original nature. Look into your original nature – experience *kensho* – and then see this embodiment as the expression of this original being.

'Satori is ever present and ever to be experienced by a simple focusing of the attention.' – Attention and awareness are the key words in Zen. Awareness is like a light in which things show themselves. 'It is known as you know yourself.' I would like to repeat that this 'knowing' pertains to the embodiment of the original nature. If one has an idea of satori as something very lofty, one is already on the wrong path. When the Buddha gave his wordless sermon in front of 500 monks, in which he held up a flower, no one understood apart from Mahakasyapa, who indicated his understanding with a quiet smile. Thereby he became the successor of the Buddha. You shouldn't harbour any grand idea about satori. To hear a tone with the ear, to glimpse an object with the eye, to pick up an object with the hand and put it down again – in these very simple acts it is to be seen.

In Zen there is a koan for beginners: 'If you call this piece of wood a stick, that is wrong; if you don't call it a stick, that is also wrong. What can you call it?' It is not something that is apart from this phenomenal world, on the contrary it stands in relation to and exists within this world of appearances. It exists simultaneously in time and space and outside of time and space.

'Ki Lou returned to his kitchen with new courage and a new dignity.' In other words, no longer with the feeling, 'I'm only a kitchen monk with the same old monotonous work every day.' But this new dignity has to be understood correctly, too. It's not about 'I'. Through Tokuzan's words, relating to the open hand, Ki Lou experienced *kensho*, and now preparing food for the other monks became an act of love. 'For when a man is aware that his past, his present and is future lie in his own hands, then, though a kitchen be his karma, he is captain of his soul.'

A monk asked his master, 'When I have nothing in my hand, what shall I do?' 'Then drop it,' replied the master. 'How can I drop it?' asked the monk. 'Then pick it up,' said the master. Fate lies in one's own hands.

THE IMPASSE

Zen is a spiritual discipline to liberate oneself from the illusions of one's own existence. What we usually assume to be and experience as reality is in a sense only imaginary. The following story deals with how to free oneself from the spell of illusions. But before I read you the story, I would like to say something by way of introduction.

Zen meditation is a form of sitting meditation called zazen. One sits with a straight back on a cushion, or if necessary, on a chair. The spine doesn't serve just to keep the physical human form upright, but it also has an inner significance. As small children we still crawl about on all fours like animals, but as consciousness develops, we gradually come to an upright position. Concomitant with this upright position, an inner development takes place which should therefore also lead to an inner uprightness.

In zazen we sit up straight and are conscious of the fact that the whole earth is underneath us. Humans don't just live on the surface of the earth, their connection to it reaches way into its depths. This connectedness is based not only on the mineral, plant and animal elements in our bodies, but also on our consciousness. The earth is our ground; in zazen we sit on it and are aware of its bearing strength. Above us is the sky with its light; and in zazen it seems as if the sky is gently resting on our shoulders. The solidity that supports us is underneath us, and the lightness is above us. Having taken up this position, one then sets up an iron wall in front of the mind, as it is traditionally expressed. One refrains from the usual fidgeting around in all kinds of thoughts, feelings, sensations and memories. Real meditation demands an inner firmness and an unwavering mind. Now to the story:

Shih Kuang was seated in meditation when Tokuzan

appeared. The latter enquired, 'How is it with the koan?'

A koan is a tool, *upaya*, that is systematically used in the Rinzai Zen School. It is a spiritual barrier that one has to pass through. It doesn't just open of itself, it is something one has to work hard for.

> Shih Kuang replied:
> 'Up against the impasse the nose is rammed,
> Fixed by an iron heel that grinds into the neck,
> It is my nose, it is my heel.
> How is that?'
> 'There, it is gone,' smiled the Master. –

Tokuzan recognised an understanding in Shih Kuang's words and continued with his questioning,

> 'What was your Koan?'
> 'What is the sound of one hand?'

This is one of the very important koans. It was formulated by Hakuin and is referred to as a 'First Barrier' koan with which one enters Zen training.

> Tokuzan asked, 'And what is the answer?'
> The monk extended his hand, 'I am cramped with much squatting. Pray help me to get up.'
> Tokuzan gripped the proffered hand and pulled him to his feet. 'Come with me to inspect my chrysanthemums,' he invited.
> He added with a certain satisfaction, 'I am proud of my blooms.'

With this he meant, 'I am proud of you.' He saw Shih Kuang as a blossom that had opened, for he had seen into his true nature. Naturally as a master Tokuzan had other monks as well whom he wanted to bring to awakening and whom he tended like precious flowers.

'Up against the impasse the nose is rammed, fixed by an iron heel that grinds into the neck....' – thus Shih Kuang describes his efforts with the koan. When one is really engaged with a koan, it's as if it was stuck in the back of one's neck. It won't leave one in peace, even at work when attending to this or that. One can't be working on the koan all the time, yet the koan is rooted there in the nape of the neck, and given half a chance, it emerges again. There is another analogy often used: it's as if one had swallowed a red-hot ball and can't spit it out again.

'It is my nose, it is my heel.' – I have to come to insight on my own, I'm my own stumbling block, I'm tripping over my own feet. In the New Testament, Jesus says, 'If thy right eye offend thee, pluck it out,' that is, if your eye stands in the way of correct seeing, then pluck it out. That is expressed very strongly, naturally symbolically, but not abstractly.

The heel and the nose have very interesting symbolical meanings. For instance, we speak of the Achilles heel, because the heel was the only vulnerable spot of the Greek hero Achilles. The feet are the foundation of life, with them we stand upon the earth. The nose, the organ of smell, is purely instinctive with animals. But with humans it goes beyond that and is also related to intuition. Figuratively we might say, 'someone has a good nose for something' or 'I smell a rat,' or 'something smells fishy', if we suspect something underhanded.

The monk said, 'It is *my* nose, it is *my* heel.' – When one realises that, then liberation begins. What ultimately hinders us is not what happens on the outside, but our own reactions to it. We usually think that this or that event in our lives is at fault, or that other people wrong us, but actually it is only how we react to circumstances and other people. Shih Kuang already knew this: 'It is my nose that is pressed against the obstacle, it is my heel that is nailed down.' He doesn't get through, but he recognises that he is the barrier. Therefore, Tokuzan said, 'There, it's gone.' With regard to this there is a very famous koan. A man came to Bodhidharma, the first Zen patriarch of China, and said,

'My spirit is troubled, please settle it for me.' Bodhidharma answered, 'Bring me your soul and I will put it to rest', whereupon the man began the search for his soul. Eventually he said, 'I can't find my soul.' Normally we place our soul somewhere inside ourselves. We say, 'My thoughts are my soul.' And we speak of a spiritual life, of a psyche. Some say the soul comes from God and is immortal, others maintain it is not immortal. In any case, everyone seems to have some kind of idea about their soul or spirit. Yet the man seeking help realised, 'I can't find my soul.' Whereupon Bodhidharma answered, 'There, I have put it to rest for you.'

There is so much in our imagination that we take to be real. These notions and ideas condition our lives both mentally and emotionally and constrain us. If we could free ourselves of these ideas, a whole different state of consciousness would come about. That is why Tokuzan said smiling, 'There, it's gone.' As soon as you realise that it is your own nose, your own heel that is hindering you, you are free.

Then Tokuzan asked which koan had pinned him down and stopped him from getting any further. It was the koan about the sound of one hand. When two hands clap together, they make a sound. But what is the sound of one hand? Many would say that it is complete nonsense because one hand doesn't make a sound. And some monks think it is quite simple and bang their hand on the table…but of course that isn't the sound of one hand. It's actually about something completely different. Two hands and their sound demonstrate the law of cause and effect. The two clapping hands are the cause, the sound is the effect. That is the duality in which we live. We always live in duality: we are strong or weak, large or small, healthy or sick, clever or stupid, good or bad, etc. But we shouldn't continuously swing back and forth in this polarity, but instead strive for oneness. What is the sound of one hand?

'The monk extended his hand. "I am cramped with much squatting. Pray help me to get up."' – That is Shih Kuang's answer. But one could also say that the existence of the hand as such is its sound. Where does this hand come from anyway? One also speaks of the hand of God when referring to creative power. The human hand shows the development of human consciousness. The thumb, across from the four fingers is characteristic of humans. Thanks to this hand humans can do what they do: handle tools, play musical instruments, write, etc. Can one not describe this activity as sound? Do we have to cling to words so heavily? Is sound something we can only perceive with the ears? Why not ask a painter or a musician; for them colours can be sounds and sounds can be colours.

'Tokuzan gripped the proffered hand and pulled him to his feet and invited him to come and inspect his chrysanthemums, and added with a certain satisfaction, "I am proud of my blooms."' – I am proud of my students when they come to an insight. This little story reveals something about the spiritual training of the Rinzai Zen School.

When speaking about self-awareness, one really must ask oneself what this 'self' actually is. Is it the body or the thoughts or the sensations or the emotions or the values according to which we orientate ourselves? One has to learn to distinguish between the true self and the illusory self. That is the first step. Then one has to liberate oneself from the illusory self. One has to, so to speak, free oneself of all clothing. We come into the world naked, and then proceed to clothe this bare body. But one shouldn't identify oneself with the clothing. Clothes have only one function. Whether one wears worker's overalls or a monk's robe or a doctor's white coat, depends on the occupation one is engaged in. But it is the same with consciousness. One clothes the naked consciousness in all kinds of apparel, and says, 'That's me.' With time, one can no longer see the naked body of consciousness, because one always remains in the same clothes. The businessman comes home at night and instead of being a husband and father, he remains a businessman. He can't change his clothes and as a consequence his wife and children are deprived of husband and father. That is only one example among many.

One has to be able to discard all clothing and stand there naked. With regard to this, it is important to understand what naked consciousness means. It is perfectly acceptable to put clothes back on, but they are only temporary roles. One shouldn't say, 'That's me, these are *my* thoughts, feelings, etc.' In any case, how do I know that they really are my thoughts? That is an assumption. It's possible, after all, that these thoughts have come from somewhere else. One reads or hears something, accepts it and makes it one's own. Thus, there are emotional garments and thought coverings, whereby one can freely take them off and put them on again. The spirit should be left free to dress one way or another depending on what the situation demands.

This freedom is achieved through two practices: correct meditation and correct understanding. Correct meditation and correct understanding are like two legs. When walking one puts down one foot after the other. I have already spoken about correct meditation today, and all of Tokuzan's tales speak about correct understanding.

Nowadays many people run to psychotherapists. They have problems with themselves, with other people or with the outside world. Then they are often told that things are very different from the way they see them. But often the clothes are only exchanged for others. In order to be truly liberated one must cease to identify with the clothing we wear. Ultimately one has to free oneself from this illusory self. This principle is known to all religions: in Christianity, in Islam, in the Indian traditions, in Buddhism, Taoism and Judaism. Each religion in their own way teaches the distinction between the true and the fictitious self.

A DARK NIGHT

On the one hand the stories about Tokuzan can be regarded as fictitious, and as such they are like the parables we find in the Bible, the Prodigal Son for example. On the other hand, these stories are not just made up, but describe actual situations. Zen stories have a very specific character. They are always aimed at experience and actualisation, as opposed to theory and speculation. Sometimes they appear to be quite rough. In that case they have the same function as when one tries to wake someone up from a deep sleep. If one quietly says, 'Wake up!' they will go on snoring. If one calls loudly, 'Wake up!', they still go on snoring. Eventually one shakes them, again to no avail. Finally, one thumps them and shouts – now they wake up. That was very rough, but it was necessary in order to get them to wake up. Some Zen stories are along these lines. The following story is called A Dark Night.

So-So was sitting in meditation when Tokuzan passed.

So-so is obviously a play on words, meaning more or less or neither good nor bad.

'Well?' said the Master raising an eyebrow.

Well, how's it going with the meditation?

'A dark night and no travellers,' said So-So.

It was dark around him and he was cold.

Rising he went towards Tokuzan and stood before him in

weary desperation. 'Master, I am cold; I could cry.'

Whirling his staff, Tokuzan sprang upon him. Caught unawares, the blow crashed home and hurt. So-So fled and furious Master and frightened disciple raced together up the road.

There is a Chinese ink drawing that depicts just such a situation, showing a master whose face is taut with anger and a disciple with an expression of great fear.

So-So had been sitting in meditation – more or less, and in response to the master's question, answered, 'A dark night and no travellers.' This 'More-or-Less So-So' is really a poor chap. In weary desperation he stands before Tokuzan. He obviously attaches great importance to this situation, but simply can't come to terms with it. Which is why he says, 'I'm so cold, I could cry.' If that's the case, then show me how cold you are and let me hear you crying, don't just talk about it! Tokuzan whirls his staff and pursues So-So through the garden.

At the other end of the road stood the monastery, and in the courtyard So-So was cornered.

In the practice of real meditation, whether it be meditation without a subject or meditation on a koan, one is driven into a corner. One *must* be driven into this corner. Sometimes life drives one into the corner. So-So could no longer escape; he could no longer escape from himself.

Panting and brushing the sweat out of his eyes he faced his pursuer.

'Are you warm? snarled Tokuzan.

Light dawned on So-So. 'I am warm,' he answered.

'Come with me,' said Tokuzan. He took So-So to the community cellar. It had no windows. 'Look down there.' So-So stood at the top of the steps and looked. A push sent him sprawling into the dark, and the door slammed to.

Now he was really in darkness. If one meditates without the light dawning on one, then one just remains in the dark, in *avidya*, in not-knowing. Meditation that doesn't result in realisation, doesn't lead to anything. Perhaps it is just an escape from oneself. That is regrettable. The human spirit should realise its true nature, one shouldn't run away from it.

Picking himself up, So-So climbed up the steps and waited by the door. Outside stood Tokuzan. 'Is it dark in there?' he asked. 'Master,' said So-So, 'It is light as day.'

Now So-So is beginning to understand something, and Tokuzan tests him:

'You lie, it is black as night.' To which So-So replies, 'Black as night to you, and light as day to me.'

In Zen this kind of verbal exchange is called *mondo* (literally: question and answer). Most koans were developed from such dialogues. *Mondo* can be occasioned by a question, a remark or a gesture. They are spontaneous encounters between master and pupil or between two masters. They are verbal exchanges which always give expression to some insight. The *mondo* in this story was triggered by So-So's assertion that it was a dark night. But when he was really pushed into darkness, he said, 'It is light as day.' 'You lie, it's black as night.' 'Black as night to you, light as day to me.'

It is no longer a question of light and dark, of day and night. There is no day without night and no night without day. This is now a transcendental matter. This *mondo* really isn't so easy to understand.

> Tokuzan opened the door, and So-So stood before him and bowed.
> 'So-So,' said the Master.
> 'Master,' said So-So.

The *mondo* ends here.

> Then Tokuzan said, 'Gently, gently goes it, little son.'

Previously he wasn't gentle at all.

> This time when So-So really wept, the Master merely smiled.

This little story shows how in Zen training insight and action belong together. Just intellectual or instinctive understanding is insufficient in Zen.

The most important part of this story is right at the end: 'So-So,' said the Master. 'Master,' said So-So. He could simply have said 'Tokuzan'. Yet because he said 'Master,' the latter said, 'Gently, gently goes it, little son.' At that So-So was deeply moved and cried. But his weeping was a happy weeping, So-So had found his way home.

At the beginning I mentioned the parable of the Prodigal Son. It tells of a rich farmer who had two sons. One of them left his home and squandered his inheritance, which he had asked to be paid out early. After he had squandered everything and landed in misery, he returned home. The father was so happy that he had a calf slaughtered and prepared a banquet.

The son returned to the father! And Tokuzan said, 'Gently, gently goes it, little son.' He was like a father to So-So. Actually, every person leaves home during their lifetime. They leave their father. Jesus told the Israelites that they should see God as a loving father. The return to the father was greatly emphasised in Christian mysticism. There is a small scripture entitled *Lambsprings*, where it describes the father, sitting on his throne, devouring his homecoming son. Father and son become one. The Christian mystic wants to become one with God, and the Indian yogi wants the self to become one with Brahman. God and the God-created soul are one. That is the 'return to the father'. One can also refer to it as the return to the True Self, which is identical to the world soul (*anima mundi*). There are many different ways of expressing this. Because man leaves his home and squanders his inheritance, it behoves him to return home. Jesus said to his disciples: 'Ye are the salt of the earth: but if the salt have lost its savour, wherewith shall it be salted?' In desert lands salt is worth gold. Without salt one gets very ill and dies. Salt is essential for life. You are the salt of the earth, but if the salt loses its flavour, wherewith can it be salted? I think Jesus was a great Zen master.

One has to return to ones innermost being, from where one has come. One has to realise that one has left one's home and squandered one's inheritance, just like Esau gave away his inheritance for a bowl of lentil soup. But on the return home, one must not longingly look back at what one has left behind. This is related in the story of Lot and his wife. God had summoned them both to turn their backs on Sodom and Gomorrah, the cities of sin and dissipation. But Lot's wife looked back and turned into a pillar of salt. Such parables can be very valuable if we try and understand them and abide by what they tell us. This little story, too, about So-So and Tokuzan is perhaps only a parable, but perhaps it also really happened.

THE SICK MONK

The next story of Tokuzan is called 'The Sick Monk'. While listening to this story one should try and put oneself in the monk's situation and in a way identify with him. Because, whether one knows it or not, one is this sick monk.

> A monk suffered from heat in the intestines. He asked Tokuzan, 'Can a man know Zen with a burning in his belly?'
> Tokuzan replied, 'Pain distorts perception, but Zen is not a matter of perception.'

One can talk about Zen and one can write about Zen. Thoughts, spoken or written words are objects. But Zen is not an object. If one says, 'I and Zen,' then two objects are standing across from one another and one finds oneself in a tricky situation. But it is nothing but an illusion. Tokuzan continued:

> 'The ignorant will ask, "What is it to us, if we may never know?" The enlightened confess that they too are ignorant. Therefore, it is said, "There is no Zen," and sages whisper, wondering, "It is true."'

When one speaks of spiritual insight, many would say, 'What's that got to do with me, I don't understand it anyway.' What is the difference between the ignorance of the unenlightened and the ignorance of the enlightened? Those who are enlightened know that they are ignorant, because reality is not a matter of perception; that is, it can neither be perceived intellectually, nor physically, nor instinctively, nor with the eyes or ears. Zen masters are very knowledgeable about many things, depending on their interests and how they were educated, but they are ignorant with respect to Zen, they don't know Zen. One could naturally ask why do they then even talk or write about Zen, if they are that ignorant about it. The reply to that would be, that there are those who speak and write about Zen and have a knowledge about Zen, and there are those who write and speak about Zen but have no knowledge of Zen. That is very paradoxical. Many years ago, when I was ordained as a teacher in Myoshin-ji, the abbot of the temple asked me, 'Will you now be writing a book about Zen?' There was no mistaking the sarcastic undertone in this question. I naturally had no such intention.

'There is no Zen,' and sages whisper, wondering, 'It is true.' – In Sino-Japanese this 'wondering' is called *myo*. It is an overwhelming wonder, awe before a great miracle. Perhaps an astronomer is amazed in the same way the first time he looks at the universe through a telescope.

> The monk was silent. In his mind was a single thought, 'Sages whisper, wondering, "It is true."'
> The thought fled, only the fragrance remained; then that too disappeared.

That happens quite often, not just when meditating on a koan, but also on other occasions. Suddenly and spontaneously an insightful thought will come to one, and the next minute it's gone again. Only an intimation lingers behind like the scent of a perfume, and this too soon evaporates.

> The monk looked at things around him and all was as before.

When one sits zazen for a long period of time one arrives at a time-and spaceless state of consciousness. When one leaves the zendo this atmosphere surrounds one like a perfume. But this fragrance evaporates and everything is as before.

One doesn't create this state of meditation, it is already there and one sinks into it like into deep water. One closes the inner eyes and ears and sinks into *samadhi*. There is a calligraphy on a folding screen in the famous Zen Temple, Nanzen-ji, which reads, 'Empty your mind and sink deep into the Tao.' After a certain amount of time, one emerges from this state again. One hears, sees and thinks, and all is as before. This is how it was for the monk in this story.

> Within was pain, and without, the window framed a blue sky. He turned to Toluzan, and beads were on his brow. Wondering, he whispered, 'It is true.'

Zen is not separate from actual existence. The moment one fabricates pictures and imagines that Zen is something special, outside of and removed from the world, one has already gone astray. After the Buddha sat all night meditating with his back against the bodhi tree, he saw the morning star at dawn and had *anuttara samyak sambodhi*, complete and perfect enlightenment. He stood up and said, 'I am Buddha.' His personal mirror-consciousness, in which the 'I' is reflected, transformed itself into the universal mirror in which everything is reflected. Buddha and the universe were one, and everything, every last thing at that moment was enlightened. This is how it is recounted. The Buddha within oneself, one's own Buddha-nature and person are one. What about that which says 'I'? When that which says 'I' is aware of its root, its origin, its source, then it knows how things stand. Lao-tzu said, 'Return to the root and nourish it.' But if this awareness is not present, then the I separates itself off, and by standing apart the world becomes a world of objects, a world of notions and divisions without an awareness of the unity.

Once when Jesus was asked who he was, he declared, 'Before Abraham was, I am.' Abraham was considered the father of the Israelites. Jesus was aware of his origin.

The story of the sick monk is an example of the Zen of the Patriarchs. In the 60s when Zen had become popular in America, through much misconstrued information, a distinction was made between 'radical' or 'square' Zen and Hippy Zen. Radical Zen is the Zen of the Patriarchs. It emphasises the necessity of freeing oneself from all erroneous views and adopting a totally different attitude towards oneself and the world. But the hippies found this too rigid and accordingly called it 'square' and wanted nothing to do with it. Because everything is Zen, they used that as a pretext for doing whatever they wanted to do. Yet the monk in this story gained his insight through, 'It is true, there is no Zen.' There is no Zen that is an object of perception. That cannot be said and emphasised often enough. Zen is a oneness. One should use one's life from day to day, from hour to hour, from minute to minute to be aware of this oneness. It is the oneness of the ten thousand things. Expressed dialectically one also speaks of oneness in multiplicity. But what does that actually mean? The Buddha observed that human consciousness is composed of five factors or aggregates. These five aggregates (*skandhas*) are: body, the senses, thoughts, tendencies and consciousness as such. These five *skandhas* form a unity, but one can be aware of them individually. We can for example be aware of the body while sitting, walking, standing and lying down. That is nothing special, it is a daily activity. Be aware of your bodies! Not necessarily of the individual positions, though that is also possible. For example, there is a meditation practice that focusses on the *chakras*. But in this complete body-awareness, the entire body is imbued by consciousness. The four positions of the body: standing, walking, sitting and lying down are four different states of consciousness.

One should also become aware of the five senses: touch, taste, smell, sound and sight. The sense of touch covers the entire surface of skin. It is the initial contact of living beings. Through this contact consciousness is called forth. If one picks something up with the hands and connects with it, consciousness and object become one. Then there is no longer any object. Everyone can verify this for themselves through personal experience. Generally, the sense of touch is experienced as the most intimate sense, more intimate than hearing or seeing. But if one cultivates hearing and seeing, these too become more intimate. For painters or musicians, colours or sounds are very intimate. Through the practice of awareness everything in our realm of perception becomes intensified. In Zen nothing new is created, no abstract notions, or objects of wishful thinking. One simply becomes aware of how reality functions in existence. When one is completely aware or this reality, one then turns one's attention to the thought streams. From the body and the senses, one now moves on to the mental formations. And after that one focuses the attention on the contents emerging from the depths of consciousness. One refers to these contents as tendencies or subconscious stirrings.

In the Theravada School, one of the earliest schools of Buddhism, a meditation technique of observation was developed, called *vipassana*. One sits and with the inner eye observes everything that appears: thoughts, physical sensations, memories, dreamlike images, etc. With this practice of observation, I-centredness is shut out. One simply observes what is present and takes no part in it. This is actually quite a natural state. If, for instance, we watch a film or read a gripping story, we also forget ourselves. What does this experience teach us? It proves that the I-less state is always present, one only needs to become aware of it.

Therefore it is important to distinguish between consciousness and its contents on the one hand, and on the other hand to experience the unity of both. Analysis and synthesis belong together. Spiritual training lies in cultivating the mirror-consciousness whereby one distinguishes between the mirror and what is reflected. And then mirror and reflection become one again. Now neither subject nor object exists, neither the one nor the other. This neither/nor is referred to as the fifth position in meditation. The first is the observation of subject and object. These are two positions together: the subject is related to the object, but the object is itself a subject and is related to an object. From this relationship between subject and object one knows that what is objective is also subjective and vice versa. This formula: subjective equals objective and objective equals subjective was already expressed by the old Taoist philosopher Chuang-tzu. In psychology this is known as a projection mechanism.

In the third position of meditation, one observes only the subjective; in the fourth position only the objective, that is, subject as subject and object as object respectively. These four positions culminate in the fifth position where there is neither subject nor object.

These five positions are very real. Everyone who practises meditation experiences them. Knowing about and experiencing these positions is absolutely essential for understanding the reality of our existence. When in our story it is said, 'It is true, there is no Zen,' then this experience corresponds to reality. It is neither philosophy, nor speculation, nor theory.

As I said at the beginning, Zen is not an object. If someone sits down and says, 'Now I want to practise Zen,' then they have already formed an idea which is just as silly as someone wanting to practise love. Love is a very natural occurrence. Either it there or not, but it can't be practised. The only thing that can be practised is awareness. The basis for this awareness is the actual, tangible body with its five sense organs through which it comes into contact with the so-called external world. Through this contact the inherent consciousness of the body is summoned out of potentiality into actuality. The sense of touch forms the basis for all the other senses. One can be born blind and deaf and can, nonetheless, develop awareness. However, if the sense of touch is missing, awareness cannot arise. Through the awakening of consciousness, thoughts, pictures and memories appear including the thoughts, feelings and tendencies that lie in the subconscious.

What happens when consciousness and object entirely become one? When Bodhidharma sat and stared at the bare wall, his spirit became one with the bare wall. With that he showed what Zen is. What is Zen? Simply that! The awareness of the unity of consciousness and its contents. In this awareness one knows nothing of Zen, and that is the ignorance of the enlightened ones. Sages whisper in awe, 'It is true.'

In many cultures cats have a special significance. In ancient Egypt a cat was considered to be holy. In some way it represented the soul. When a cat sits in front of a mouse hole, it is completely calm and relaxed and doesn't take its eyes off the mouse hole for a moment. Now and again its tail quivers slightly. Yet the moment the mouse shows itself, it pounces. This deportment is a good analogy for Zen meditation. Sit calm, relaxed and alert! One shouldn't sit all tensed up with clenched teeth. Meditation is a sinking into oneself, not a descent into unconsciousness, but rather an alert, clear and lucid awareness, just like the cat in front of the mouse hole.

Sokei-an had a cat. It was quite an ordinary cat, but it had no tail. During our zazen in Sokei-an's room – we had no zendo like here, we simply sat on chairs because there wasn't enough space for mats and cushions – the cat would sometimes come in. It didn't say 'miao' or rub itself against people's feet; it simply strolled up and down and observed the sitters. Then it would jump on that person's lap whose meditation was deepest and there it remained, seated calm and motionless. At the end of the meditation, it would leave again. This is really what happened. And the following story about Tokuzan is also about a cat:

> Tokuzan was about to give a sermon. He looked past the assembly of monks to where a kitten was at play in the further corner of the hall. He said, 'The Way of Heaven is to walk in Tao.'

In the *Tao-te-ching* it says, 'Man models himself on earth, the earth models itself on heaven, heaven models itself on the Tao and the Tao models itself on its own inherent nature.' A newly born human being is first and foremost shaped by earthly things. Everything revolves around its physical living existence. That is why the earth is the model for human beings. The model for the earth is heaven. Without heaven the earth would be lifeless. The sun and the moon play a vital role in the life of the earth. The model of heaven is the Tao, and the Tao obeys its own inherent nature. But not in the same way as humans who make their own 'I' as their model. After human beings are born into this world, that which is no longer completely earthly begins to develop with time. Their activities are no longer confined to just eating, drinking and physical movement. Through the body and its senses consciousness is stimulated and humans become aware of their existence. Though their feet are bound to the earth by gravity, their eyes are directed towards the firmament of heaven. This awareness of themselves and their environment is something spiritual. It goes beyond what is earthbound and is oriented towards things in heaven. Because the Tao is the model for heaven, those who are oriented towards heaven, that is those who live the spiritual aspect of their lives, walk the way of the Tao. Tokuzan continues:

'What is this Tao? It is the nature of all things.'

'All things' are not just the inanimate objects we usually regard as things, but also living, sentient beings. They too are things.

'And what is the nature of things? It is the principle of pleasure, to seek after what you like and to recoil from what you dislike.'

Is Tokuzan speaking about the pleasure principle from a Freudian point of view? We shall soon find out.

Tokuzan descended from the pulpit and walked over to where the kitten was playing with a ball of silken thread. Trailing the thread on the floor he enticed the kitten on to the pulpit, and there all watched it continue its game.

Tokuzan turned to the monks and said, 'Life can be pleasurable. Union with pleasure is pleasurable. Separation from the unpleasant is pleasurable. Any craving that is satisfied, that is also pleasurable. Pleasure is caused by craving. Pleasure more abundant is caused by cultivating the art of craving....'

The Buddha said that the greatest obstacle to the deliverance from suffering is the craving linked to the realm of form and names (*rupadhatu*). Therefore, one should renounce all craving and return to the form-and nameless realm (*arupadhatu*). In a verse of Lao-tzu we read, 'There is something formless, soundless, and colourless, and that cannot be scrutinised any further.' Yet Tokuzan has just said that 'pleasure more abundant is caused by cultivating the art of craving,' But now he continues,

'The way to cultivate this art is the Eightfold Path.'

With that he is referring to the Buddha's teaching about suffering and the way out of suffering.

In the later Mahayana Buddhist teaching of the *trikaya*, one distinguishes three bodies of the Buddha (in Sanskrit *trikaya* means three bodies). These are called *dharmakaya, sambhogakaya* and *nirmanakaya*. The *nirmanakaya* is the transformation body, the manifested body. The *sambhogakaya* is the body of unity. Sometimes it is also referred to as the body of enjoyment because the state of unity is a state of harmony in which there are no opposites and consequently no conflicts. But this viewpoint is related to humans. The word 'Dharma' has many different meanings. The *dharmakaya* is usually translated as the body of the law. One could also say the body of natural law, whereby this is not nature as it is usually thought of, but nature in the wider sense. It is the principle underlying everything.

The Dharma-body contains the joy of life. How does this joy of life find expression? Who can give a good answer to this question? At the moment we are sitting in this room. What do we hear? Outside the birds are chirping. The zendo is situated on a noisy thoroughfare. Do you hear the man-made noises or do you hear the sounds of nature? Do you hear the birds? Birds have a morning and evening song. That is their expression of the joy of life in the *dharmakaya*. That is only a small example of the joy of living in this existence. Every living thing wants to live; the gratification of this wanting is pleasure. Tokuzan says, 'Pleasure is caused by cultivating the art of craving.' This is a very simple matter: craving can focus on the external world, where according to Lao-tzu only the outer shell of things is seen. It is pleasurable to possess this or that. However, if one loses it, it is no longer a pleasure. Jesus said that one shouldn't acquire treasures that thieves will steal or that moths will eat, but invest in the treasures of heaven. So, craving can go in a worldly direction, but it can also move towards the spiritual and become an inner yearning for true insight. With that an intimation that there is something that goes beyond the transient things of this earth begins to grow along with a yearning for it. In Christian mysticism this is referred to as the search for the Beloved. One longs for the mystical marriage through the union with the Beloved. Because it is inherent in human consciousness to be able to distinguish between the spiritual and the material, it can also search for the union of these two. But first the one has to separated from the other, only then can it come to a union.

Initially an unconscious oneness exists, also called chaos. This is followed by the separation of spirit and matter, and then there is a new union. That is the basic principle underlying all paths to enlightenment. Even the spagyric art of the alchemists is based on this. In daily life this is happening constantly. It gives us pleasure when the ear hears a beautiful sound, the eye sees a pleasing form or colour, the palate tastes something delicious and the sense of touch feels something pleasant. The body takes in light through the eyes, air through the lungs and nourishment through the stomach. These are all procedures of unification. In yoga consciously becoming one with an object is called *samjana*. Both in Indian as well as in Buddhist tantric yoga, unification is understood in the context of a spiritual path.

Tokuzan said that cultivating the art of craving is called the Eightfold Path, but then he continues,

'I call the path "Right Play."'

Just observe how a small child, that is not yet burdened with the habits and fixed ideas of adults, plays. It finds itself in a wonderful world. One can call it the magical phase. This early child is still very much connected with the *dharmakaya*. That is reflected in its playing. Adults can no longer play in this way. But there are some people who haven't lost this connection with the early child within themselves. Something plays in them. A good example is Albert Einstein, a simple person who opened up a new world for us. He was a genius. Those who knew him had the pleasure of experiencing this veritable primordial child (Urkind) in him.

'Right Play'! One could argue that it is a serious matter to walk the way to enlightenment, a way that is straight and narrow and from which one may not deviate. How can such strict discipline be play if one has to really exert oneself like a businessman who wants to earn a lot of money, or an artist who wants to perfect his masterpiece for an exhibition? No, this way is not an I-centred undertaking. It is the very innermost being in us, the child Jesus or the Buddha-child, that has to walk this way. The latter stood up right after his birth and pointing to heaven and earth said, 'Throughout the world I alone am the World-honoured One.' What does this mean? What is actually implied with this Buddha-child whose birthday is still celebrated today by pouring tea over a small upright standing figure with one hand pointing to heaven and the other to earth? What is this primordial child, this very innermost being? There are different koans to help one understand this. It is not enough to be told, 'This child is in you, it has just been buried under all the layers of responsibility and values you have acquired as an adult.' One has to truly encounter this child. It shouldn't just remain an idea, like in the German song, 'How blissful, how blissful to still be a child'.

> Tokuzan continued, 'When a Zen monk travels the path in question, I see a dragon beating its wings in trackless wastes, gambolling with the spirits of the upper airs.'

In China the dragon is a very important symbol. There are many illustrations in which a dragon emerges from deep water, soars into the air and spewing fire plays with a pearl. That is the Cloud Dragon. His domain is the trackless wasteland.

We live in this world and leave behind footprints, and our feet take on the dust of the earth. Yet there is a sphere in which no traces are left behind. The dragon gambols with the spirits of the upper airs. That is truly playing! We dance with the spirits of the lower airs, but we do not see them as spirits. We think they have a real existence. Our ideas, for instance, are such spirits. However, they are not located in the sphere of the trackless wastes.

Tokuzan continued, 'How now, monks? I ask you, how should a Zen monk play?'

Those of you who have spent time in a monastery know that Zen training in a monastery is very demanding and the discipline rigorous. How and when are monks supposed to play? This doesn't imply that everything one does should effortlessly and playfully fall into place or that now and then one allows oneself a ballgame.

Tokuzan brandished his staff of office, 'Here is a stick. If there be a dragon among the chickens, let him fly forth and scorch this tree with his fiery breath.'

Tokuzan called all of his monks chickens, and that's also how they behaved. On the basis of their ideas they lay eggs and cluck, 'I have understood something...' 'If there is a dragon among the chickens, let him fly forth and scorch this tree.' – Suddenly the stick is a tree. Naturally it is a tree. If you call this stick a stick, it is completely wrong, but if you don't call it a stick, that is also wrong. What can you call it? So perhaps you call it a tree. Then show me this tree. Now you stand there completely bewildered.

So-So stepped forward and took the stick from Tokuzan's hand. He trailed it out of the hall and into the garden, with the kitten falling over his feet.

Tokuzan had taken a silk thread and enticed the kitten onto the pulpit. Now So-So takes the stick and the cat goes with him.

The Master shook his head and said, 'Was ever a teaching so misinterpreted?' But he smiled as a man amused.

When a Zen master sees that a student has really passed through a barrier, when some obstacle has fallen off like a burden and he comes to an insight, then he is truly pleased. The teacher is strict and urges the student to exert himself and awakens in him a desire for realisation. And when the student attains it, he rejoices with him.

This discipline that one imposes on oneself – practising zazen, controlling one's thoughts, working in great heat and also in freezing temperatures and on top of that in the Rinzai school working with koans – that is all quite tough. So where is the play? So-So has just shown us how the dragon in the trackless wastes gambols with the spirits of the upper airs. Only the primordial child, if one lets it play, can express it in such a way, like So-So the dragon. Tokuzan led the kitten onto the pulpit with him and So-So took it into the garden with him. Tokuzan at the pulpit, So-So in the garden.

In the end this whole episode really concerns the kitten, and because it is about a cat, I want to tell you about the famous koan that also deals with a cat: two groups of monks were having an argument. One group said that the cat in the temple belonged to the monks and the other group said it belonged to the temple. The great master Nansen by chance overheard this and at the next assembly he took the cat by the scruff of the neck and held it up, saying, 'If one of you can say who this cat really belongs to, he can save the cat's life. If no one can say the true word, I will cut its head off.' None of the monks could say who the cat really belonged to and so the cat lost its life. The next day the monk Joshu returned from a journey. He would later become the great master to whom the 'Mu-koan' is attributed. Nansen related what had happened to the cat. After Joshu had listened, he said not a word. He simply took his sandals off, placed them on his head and left the room. Thereupon Nansen said, 'Oh, Joshu, if you had been here, you could have saved the cat's life.'

Now with koans it's not a matter of just having ideas about what is written in the scriptures and the sutras, but to break through to genuine insight oneself. One shouldn't get stuck with just the ideas in the head. Anyone can have ideas, words are cheap and paper doesn't blush.

Tokuzan said, 'Was ever a teaching so misinterpreted?' But he smiled, showing his pleasure. And that is typically Zennish. Zen masters intentionally behave paradoxically; for the truth is paradoxical. The master says, 'You don't understand anything, you are the biggest fool I have ever come across,' and laughs. And conversely, 'Oh yes, you understand, you're an amazing fellow. Now make yourself scarce. Don't poison the air here with your understanding.'

> My master scolded me – his love is great.
> My master praised me – he's a mean old guy.

The following story is a good example of a *mondo*. Its title is 'The Rose Bush'.

> The priest T'zun was versed in Tao, and felt that he was free.

One refers to someone who has realised Tao as free. Free from what? Free from themselves. He lives in Tao. The word 'Tao' has different meanings. On the one hand it can mean 'way' in the sense of 'method', but on the other hand it can also mean 'truth'. It depends on the context in which it is used.

> Having heard of Tokuzan by repute, one day he called on the master to test his knowledge.

It is not clear here, whether T'zun wanted to test Tokuzan's knowledge or test his own knowledge. In *sanzen* the student tests his own knowledge before the teacher, and if he then has true insight, real *satori*, he can also test his teacher. Such encounters can sometimes be very interesting. They are a kind of combat, spiritual Judo, so to speak.

> Tokuzan was engaged in pruning the rose bushes. After ceremonial greetings had been exchanged, T'zun said, 'Let us talk of Tao.' 'I know nothing of Tao,' replied the Master, 'you tell me.'

The old Taoists say that those who speak about the Tao or ask about it, haven't got an inkling about the Tao. They might just have ideas in the head. So, Tokuzan said 'I know nothing about the Tao.

You tell me about it.' Thereupon T'zun replied:

'In Tao water becomes oil and stone turns into gold.'

That is an interesting remark. On the one hand there is the old, pure Taoism as represented by Lao-tzu, and on the other hand numerous deviations of an esoteric nature. One of these deviations is Taoist alchemy, another is tantric Taoism. In alchemy one concerns oneself with the transformation of base substances into noble substances. For instance, lead is transformed into gold. Though the alchemists did try in very concrete tangible processes to transform lead into gold, there was also another deeper meaning involved in this practice. Lead symbolises the saturnine aspect of man with his karmic conditioning; that is not a noble state.

Transformation into gold symbolises the spiritual development in which one attempts to reach the inner light and realises the true self. It is a transformation of consciousness from a personal conditioned identity to the true self, from Saturn to the sun. 'When one realises Tao, water becomes oil and stone turns to gold,' said T'zun, who felt that he was free. In the Catholic Church one is baptised with water and confirmed with oil.

Tokuzan said, 'In truth water remains water and stone remains stone.'

Though he said, 'In truth…' it is better to say 'in reality'. It is important to make the philosophical differentiation between reality and truth. The world of phenomena is a reality, a moving force. Perhaps what is above and beyond that could be said to be truth.

'I should have explained,' the priest hastened to assure him, 'that only the essence changes; the form remains the same.'

During the celebration of Catholic Mass, the wine becomes the blood of Jesus, the bread his body. Viewed theologically, the form remains the same, but the essence is changed. This way of looking at things goes back to Aristotle who made the distinction between form and matter. Aristotle is the father of our Western science. Correspondingly T'zun says, 'I should have explained that only the essence changes, the form remains the same.'

> 'May I ask how you know?' enquired Tokuzan.
> 'By this (Tao),' said the priest proudly, as one who has said the last word.

This goes back to the *Tao-te-ching* where Lao-tzu asks himself, 'How do I know that the Tao is like it is?', at which he answers himself, 'I know it by THIS.'

> Tokuzan pointed at the rose bush he had been pruning and asked, 'What is this?'
> 'A rose bush,' answered T'zun.
> 'Oh! Master Magician, what is this?' he asked again.
> T'zun hesitated. 'I see what you mean. I do not know.'

Perhaps T'zun took a step forward with this answer, but Tokuzan doesn't accept it. He could have carried on with, 'Why don't you know?' but instead he said,

> 'Oh, child, breaker of cauls, what is that?'

A caul is the amniotic membrane that surrounds some newborn

babies and must be broken open. In the folk tradition a child born with this so-called 'veil' is said to have the gift of second sight.

> T'zun stared at the shrub. Then, 'It is Tao.'
> 'It's a rose bush,' said Tokuzan.
> T'zun was relieved. 'We are agreed. In essence all is one.'

This statement finds its strongest theoretical underpinning in the philosophy of the Avatamsaka School of Buddhism or Kegon-shu as it is called in Japanese. In terms of Western physics one would say that all manifested forms can be reduced to energy and therefore ultimately are all one. T'zun advocates this thought when he says, 'In essence all is one.' Tao is the essence.

> 'I said, it is a rose bush,' repeated Tokuzan.
> Agitated, T'zun sprang to his feet. 'What miserable magic is this? Would you give so much and then take it all?'

Tokuzan had said that a rose bush is a rose bush. T'zun was relieved, for he thought they were of the same opinion. Yet now Tokuzan says that it is only a rose bush and nothing more. T'zun is confused and angry, he no longer knows where he stands. 'Would you give so much and then take it all?' When one has grasped something intellectually or emotionally, it almost becomes an intellectual or emotional possession. And that, one latches onto. From a Zen point of view, but also from a Taoist standpoint, this possession must be relinquished. I experienced this myself. At the age of sixteen I read the esoteric novel *The Green Face* by Gustav Meyrink and subsequently became his pupil. Gustav Meyrink used to explain everything to me in the most wondrous manner. He would create magnificent thought constructions, and when I thought, 'Ah, now I understand

– I understand existence, understand myself, understand the whole world, understand the meaning of the universe, etc.' Whenever I thought, 'Now I have grasped it', then Meyrink would systematically go about destroying it. He continued to do this again and again until I realised that thought constructions don't always correspond to reality, and that one cannot under any circumstances rely on them to correspond to the truth. One realises the same thing when working with koans. One believes one has penetrated a koan and has realised something. In one sense this is true, but from another perspective, it is not so. T'zun is therefore flustered, 'Would you give so much and then take it all away again?'

This giving and taking has to be understood really well. In Zen one says, 'Let go of me with both hands.' In that moment when you are holding something, you are not free. You are held by what you are holding on to. That applies at all levels – physical, mental and emotional. To T'zun's complaint Tokuzan replies,

'I have told you I know nothing of Tao, but here is a rose bush.'

On the one hand the statement that in essence everything is one is correct, but on the other hand it is a simple way out. It is a rose bush!

Putting his hands together, the priest bowed to the Master.
'I am not your equal. What would you advise?'
'Feed your lambs.'
'And how?'
Tokuzan shrugged. 'You see, you know, you say.'
T'zun rose to depart. He said, 'I shall teach them that in Tao water becomes oil, and stone turns to gold.'
'Flowers will grow in profusion,' said Tokuzan, and he

bowed to the priest.

This is a superb *mondo*. 'Feed your lambs.' 'How?' 'You see, you know, you say.' Simple, just like that. 'I shall teach them – these lambs (!) – that in Tao water becomes oil and stone turns to gold.'

> After T'zun had gone, Tokuzan snipped another branch of his bush. Then he took brush and ink, and wrote this reflection in verse:
>
> > To prune roses is good,
> > To prune a priest is better.
> > Cut off his head,
> > Then his heart will speak.

Much more could be said about this story, but it clearly points to what is important. On the one hand the Tao, on the other hand the world of phenomena; on the one hand reality with its many different forms, and on the other hand absolute truth. Expressed in epistemological terms the phenomenal world is an objectification of the noumenal world. The noumenon is the substance, the essence from which the world of appearances, the phenomenal world is objectified. This is how it can be regarded and discussed philosophically, but to carry it over into daily life, to actual-ise it, that is another matter. For this the following koan is often used: 'You see an object. Is it inside or outside? Does this object exist outside of your consciousness or within your consciousness?' The student has to find the answer himself.

Every object we see is seen in a very specific way, because we have a specific kind of eye. If we had compound eyes like many insects have, then we wouldn't see the same object as one object, but as many different ones. So, how is this to be understood? Is the thing the object, and my consciousness the subject? The object exists 'as such', but naturally I do not know what it is 'as such'. Therefore, my picture of it is subjective. Now, is the object outside or inside my consciousness? When I was young there was a period in Berlin where the question whether everything was subjective or whether everything was objective exercised many minds. In Zen meditation this is also something one concerns oneself with. (See the discussion on the four positions in the previous chapter.) Eventually one experiences the state where there is neither subject nor object. But this experience during meditation should also spill over into our daily lives, into our relationship with others and with things and with ourselves.

The rose bush is a rose bush. But the rose bush is also Tao. Don't cling to any intellectual or intuitive definition, let go and see what really is. This giving and taking is the core of the present story.

Before I go into this story, I would like to make a few comments in relation to charity.

Jesus said, 'I have not come to abolish the law, but to fulfil it.' Then he added the eleventh commandment to augment the ten commandments of Moses. It reads: 'Love thy neighbour as thyself.'

The charity of which Jesus speaks rests on the love of people towards God and God's love of humanity and is figuratively depicted as the Sacred Heart of Jesus. This heart is pictured in the middle of the chest, not on the left side where the physical heart is located. The position of the heart of Jesus in the middle corresponds to the heart *chakra* of the Indian traditions. It is also comparable to the compassionate heart in Buddhism known as *karuna*. Every human being should become aware of this loving and compassionate heart.

Buddha was a prince. He lived a luxurious life and was shielded from all things unpleasant and unsightly. He only knew of the beautiful within the palace. Yet one day he stepped outside the palace and encountered a poor person, a sick person and a corpse. All of this he had never seen before. That touched his heart so deeply that he left the palace and his family and became a mendicant monk. He told himself that he needed to find out why poverty, sickness and death existed. And so his search for insight began. After a number of years, during a long night in meditation under the bodhi tree, he discovered his Buddha-nature. At the sight of the morning star his eye opened. He stood up and said, 'I am Buddha.' He attained the state of nirvana and from then on made it his goal to show people how to attain this liberating state. He said, every human being is bewildered, goes astray and thus suffers. Through the realisation of the truth, one is freed from this confusion.' Jesus also said, 'Abide in me and you shall know the truth and the truth shall make you free.'

On the one hand you have the sacred heart of Jesus and on the other the compassionate heart of the Buddha. In both cases the power lies at the centre of the heart. In this connection I might mention that there are three main centres of consciousness in the human body: first of all, the heart centre, second the point between the eyebrows – in images of the Buddha a jewel is often placed here – and thirdly the area around the naval, known as *hara* in Japanese. To cultivate this heart centre is the aim of Indian Bhakti-yoga. Bhakti means devotion, and implied is devotion to the divine abiding in the heart centre. Bhakti-yoga is closely related to Karma-yoga, the yoga of action.

In the Indian tradition a second important emphasis is placed on Jnana-yoga, the yoga of realisation and knowledge. Out of this the pure meditation of Raja-yoga arose. Bhakti-yoga, Karma-yoga, Jnana-yoga and Raja-yoga are the four principal paths of yoga from the ancient Indian tradition. Actually, there are only two because Raja- and Jnana-yoga and Bhakti- and Karma-yoga, respectively belong together. I only mention this in order to point out that the Indian tradition as well as the Buddhist and Christian traditions essentially have the same emphasis and the same purport.

In Buddhism two great schools developed. It seems that what later emerged as Mahayana Buddhism, at some point split off from the original Buddhism known as Theravada or School of the Elders. Mahayana means 'Great Vehicle'. In Theravada the focus is on the concept of the arhat, a worthy one. According to this principle, a monk climbs out of the vale of tears up to the mount of realisation from where he has a clear view into all of nature and the emptiness beyond the attachments to forms. And with that his path has been completed. In the Mahayana the 'Bodhisattva Ideal' developed. According to this understanding one makes one's way to the mountain summit as in the

Theravada approach and is liberated from human delusions, but then one returns to the valley and brings this realisation to people.

That is the function of a bodhisattva. *Sattva* means essence, *bodhi* means wisdom. The bodhisattva has attained the essence of wisdom and spreads this among people. He does exactly what the Buddha did after he saw into his true nature and returned to live among people. Instead of keeping his insight for himself, he spent 49 years until his death teaching. Everyone should be a bodhisattva. It is the same with the charitableness taught by Jesus. 'Love your neighbour as yourself,' applies to everyone. Naturally it has to be understood what is meant by this love of self. It is not a narcissistic, egocentric state, quite the contrary. If one cannot love oneself, if one is in conflict with oneself, that is being at odds with oneself, then one is not able to be charitable. I am speaking of true brotherly love, not something that is advantageous to oneself, in the sense of, 'If I do this for you, then I will get this in return.'

To love oneself really means to accept oneself. Here we have to go beyond the purely psychological. It is generally accepted today that humans suffer from internal conflicts. They are divided, split beings. They cannot accept themselves and are constantly looking for love that will prove to them that they are acceptable to others. Jesus knew that humans really don't possess self-love. Since then, nothing has changed, people are still exactly the same. That is why he said we should regard God as a loving father and not just as a chastising father. One can love a loving father. It is the same love of God as we saw in the Indian Bhakti-yoga. Through this love one can realise one's own true nature as a child of God. In the recognition and acceptance of this true being is where self-love is found, a self-love that does not search for selfish advantages. This self-love rests in the realisation of *tat tvam asi* – thou art that. That is relevant to everyone. You are not different from me, and I am not different from you.

Therefore, if we are all children of God, endowed with the same divine breath, then we are all one. But only if we truly realise this true being in ourselves, do we know that it is the same in everyone. That is why the Indians greet one another with folded hands and a bow, which expresses, 'I greet your true self.' Love of others arises out of true self-love. As long as one exists in a split, confrontational state, there can be no love, only fear reigns.

We usually contrast love and hate. But hate is not really the opposite of love. What is really the obverse of love is fear. Fear arises from hate, as does envy and jealousy. That is why Jesus said that love dispels fear. One is afraid of all kinds of things: fear of others, fear of death, etc. That results in insecurity, hate, jealousy, etc. I repeat: love dispels fear.

The ancient Greeks distinguished three kinds of love: *eros, agape,* and *philia*, that is physical love, brotherly love and totally impersonal love. For example, philosophy (*philia*) is the love of wisdom (*sophia*). What would one correspondingly call the love of God? I use the word 'God' here as the essence of true existence – the love of God would be *theophilia*. It is a transpersonal love.

As you can see the word 'love' has many meanings and we should be more careful about how we use it. The charity or brotherly love that is being discussed here goes beyond the personal. It encompasses *agape, eros* and *philia*. It is an all-embracing, all-pervasive love. Now we can come to today's story.

> Lu had spent the evening in the company of his friends. Returning alone to his dwelling, a strange sickness overcame him, like to nothing he had ever known.

That can happen to us every now and again. We were among friends and it was very pleasant and perhaps very stimulating, and then we are suddenly overcome by a strange feeling. But it is not an illness brought on by too much alcohol.

He cried aloud in his pain, and the cry was, 'Let it be born!'
Marvelling greatly, he commemorated the occasion in verse:

> Sweet in my ear is the conversation with friends;
> Sweet in my heart is the cry of the uncreate;
> I rock to and fro in the rhythm of my travail;
> Let it be born! Let it be born!

Later he sought out Tokuzan and asked him to explain the meaning of the experience. 'Do good unto others,' was the answer, and the Master would say no more.

Lu was indignant. This monk, for all his repute, was a common priest capable only of platitude. Bowing with scant respect he departed, and the Master watched him go. 'Nor self, nor others, not even the Buddha,' he reflected as the visitor disappeared.

In the following week Lu was again returning from one of his visits in which he delighted. The way led through a wood, and without warning a rotten branch fell with a crash, barely missing the man. Lu was startled beyond measure, and simultaneously he became enlightened. Making up his mind on the spot, he went straight to the monastery.

Tokuzan was taking the air before retiring. His feet made tracks in the dewy grass; his eyes were on the moon. Lu accosted him without preamble:

> 'I must do good to others!
> Difficult it is indeed.
> Going forth I find no others;
> Returning there is no trace, not even of myself.'

'Nor self, nor others, not even the Buddha,' the Master agreed.

'I now perceive that charity is indeed an art,' said Lu.

'Comparable only to the virtue of conversation between

friends,' said Tokuzan, drawing him into step.

That is a very nice story, but is its meaning at all comprehensible? Perhaps it is possible in the light of what I was talking about in the beginning.

In the Bible it says that man should not live alone. Human beings are social beings. Even if from time to time they stand apart by withdrawing into a forest hut to meditate, they are still companionable beings and reliant on others. But what usually takes place in social gatherings, we know well enough. Through associating with others, one usually tries to come closer to oneself and that brings about many difficulties. Lu, too, had spent such an evening in companionship with friends. But then as he was returning home – alone – one has to realise that man is alone, even if that isn't good – he was overcome by a strange feeling. The aloneness which is mentioned here is a cutting oneself off from one's self. If one believes that one can emerge from this self-centred isolation by associating with others, then one is mistaken. One has to go somewhere else in order to come out of one's self.

Lu had never before experienced this strange sickness. He was used to spending his time with friends. From where then did this sickness suddenly come? He cried aloud, 'Let it be born!' What should be born? – Love should be born, and namely that love from which charity comes forth. If you and I are one in every respect, then one no longer is alone. The true self has the same nature in everyone. Buddha-nature, Purusha, Atman, God, however one wants to call it, it is the same in everyone, there is no difference; we all labour under the same delusion, there are only variations on the same theme. For this reason, Jesus said, 'See the beam in your own eye and not the speck of dust in the eye of your neighbour.' Extremely amazed, Lu put his experience into a verse:

'Sweet in my ear is the conversation of friends
Sweet in my heart is the cry of the uncreate
I rock to and fro in the rhythm of my travels...'

This travelling back and forth between friends is a journey. But there is still another journey, it is the journey of the veritable return. Meant is not the return to one's own dwelling, but the return to the truth.

'Let it be born!' Let the love be born that comes from the realisation of the truth and out of which charity arises.

Later Lu sought out Tokuzan and asked his advice. 'Do good unto others,' was the answer. Lu found this answer banal and was indignant. 'This monk, for all his high repute was just a common priest only capable of platitudes. With scant respect he bowed and departed.'

'The following week when Lu was again returning home from visiting friends, a rotten branch fell directly at his feet. Lu was startled beyond measure and was immediately enlightened.' – In that instant he realised his true self. There are a number of examples in Zen where just such a shock, brought about by some kind of incident, leads to realisation. Sokei-an came across a dead horse in the street and in that moment experienced *anuttara samyak sambodhi* – supreme perfect enlightenment. And that at the sight of a dead horse! He immediately returned to his teacher in Japan who confirmed his enlightenment. Or there was the monk who was absorbed in sweeping the garden when a pebble struck a bamboo and went 'ping' – and at that moment he was awakened.

A master had a pupil who simply couldn't understand anything. Finally, he led him to a precipice and asked the same crucial question, and when he still couldn't answer, he pushed him into the abyss. The pupil cried out in horror, and in that moment, he realised the truth.

Such stories are told.

Rinzai always had his stick to hand. He was very temperamental and impatient and hit his students at every opportunity, shouting 'Kwatz!' With that he meant, 'Wake up! Wake up!' Enlightenment, liberation, satori, are all different words for awakening. Under the terms enlightenment and satori one can create all kinds of pictures, but it is quite clear what awakening is. Either one is awake or one is not awake. Be awake, don't sleep! Lu awoke through his fright. Not everyone wakes up when they get a fright. Something has to precede this shock. When it is present, that is, if it is ripe, then it needs no more than a prod and it is born. St. Paul said, that we are like seeds, but only seeds sown in the soil will produce fruit. The seed is there, but it must be cultivated to maturity.

Many years ago, when Ruth Sasaki, an American Buddhist, first went to Japan to study Zen, she went to the great Master Nanshinken of Nanzen-ji Temple. This was in the days before Westerners and hippies travelled East. Master Nanshinken said she could start Zen training, but not immediately. He advised her to take a room and to sit for one year with *mu. Mu* means 'no' or 'nothing'. When meditating with *mu*, everything one encounters is met with a '*mu*'. Ruth Sasaki had already practised yoga, so she knew how to sit. So she sat for a year with *mu*, and when the year was up she returned to Nanshinken, who immediately recognised that she had reached the ground of the truth. She was then admitted to training together with the Japanese monks. I only mention this to show that the inner being has to be slowly matured. In order for it to ripen it has to be cared for as one would tend and nourish a seed and small plant. That is why Lao-tzu advised returning to the root and nourishing it.

'Making up his mind on the spot, Lu returned to the monastery.' – It was exactly the same with Sokei-an. He always had a ship's ticket at hand, airplane travel wasn't common then. And as soon as he had his experience, he immediately went from New York back to his teacher, Sokatsu, in Japan.

'Tokuzan was just taking the air before retiring. His feet made tracks in the dewy grass; his eyes were on the moon. Lu accosted him without preamble. "I must do good to others! Difficult it is indeed. Going forth, I find no others. Retuning, there is no trace, not even of myself."' – And now for the second time Tokuzan says, 'Neither self, nor other, not even the Buddha.' – What is the difference to the first time he uttered this sentence? The first time it was said to the departing unenlightened Lu, the second time to the returning enlightened Lu. With the words, 'Going forth, I find no others and returning, I find no trace...,' Lu had shown his enlightenment.

'"I now perceive that charity is indeed an art,"' said Lu. "Comparable only to the virtue of conversation with friends," said Tokuzan, drawing him into step.' – Why is charity an art in comparison with conversations with friends? The former is the awareness of one's self, the latter is the idle chatter with oneself and others. Tokuzan was catching a breath of fresh air, his gaze was on the moon and his feet were leaving traces in the dewy grass. This was not idle chatter! His reality left behind traces in the moist grass. There is an enormous difference between the all-encompassing Self and all these various acquaintances. In the *Bhagavad-Gita* Krishna refers to Arjuna's relatives as enemies. He orders Arjuna to fight against these enemies. But Arjuna says, 'How can I fight against them, when they are my friends and acquaintances?' Yet Arjuna has to recognise who these enemies actually are and do battle with them. They are the enemies within ourselves. Nowadays, from a psychological point of view, one would say that it is what one projects of oneself onto the outside and then sees in others instead of in oneself. These projections have to be fought in order to realise one's own true being.

Without the charity, that arises out of the realisation and acceptance of one's own self, friends, relations and acquaintances are enemies. But Lu had realised his great No-Self: 'Going forth, I find no traces, not even of myself.' As long as one is still in the state of differentiations, then no unity can be present. But now Lu could understand Tokuzan's words: 'Neither self, nor others, not even Buddha.' He was no longer stuck in the object-subject-relationship. There is a Zen saying, which might seem quite blunt: 'In front of the Buddha I bow, behind him, I give him kick.' Now Lu can say, 'I perceive that charity is indeed an art.' It is the art of seeing the true self in everyone.

THE OLD WOMAN

Old women play a significant role in Zen literature. There are several koans about old women. Young women, too, have a certain meaning, but the significance of the old woman is something very different.

> Tokuzan was out early, gathering herbs on the mountain. He saw a lonely hut and called to beg for rice. At his knock the door was opened by an old woman who prostrated herself at the sight of the robe. 'Pray be seated,' she said, 'and I will fill your bowl.'

Every monk owns his own robe and his own bowl. The robe shows that the respective person is a monk or a nun and the bowl is a sign of poverty. 'I will fill your bowl.' Do you understand what the old woman is saying? The whole monk is a begging bowl and in order to fill it, it needs to be empty.

So Tokuzan entered the hut, sat down and ate.

Realistically seen, the stomach also needs to be empty so that it can be filled and nourish one. And the lungs too need to be empty in order to gather in the breath. The living principle of breathing is a continual emptying, filling and emptying again. If the stomach isn't emptied, one gets sick; if the lungs aren't emptied, one suffocates. But it seems that emptying needs to be learned, because we tend to want to keep everything. What happens if the heart/mind (Geist) isn't emptied? For you have to know that there is also something like an empty heart/mind.

'What do you do here?' asked Tokuzan when he had eaten.
'I live alone,' said the woman. 'No one comes to visit me. I grow vegetables and sell them in the village to buy rice.'

This old woman lives alone. This aloneness is also something that is very important. In the *Tao-te-ching* it is said, that those who live in harmony with the Tao are alone. Many people nowadays complain about being isolated, so they seek relationships with others or to communicate with nature. Closeness to nature can be an enhancement. But one remains alone in a vast spaciousness. Jesus spent forty days in the wilderness to be alone with himself. But most people don't want to be alone like that. They feel lonely and forlorn and look for the company of others, and the others also don't want to be alone and abandoned. But here the situation is different. The woman is alone without delving into the contents of all kinds of things – the contents of her world of thoughts or the contents of her surroundings. That is the aloneness of a person who lives in harmony with the Tao or as it says in the Bible: 'Foxes have their dens and birds have their nests, but the Son of Man has nowhere to lay his head.' This aloneness is not an encapsulation in one's own I, but rather it is an inner collectedness in everything one does. One doesn't go into a zendo or monastery and practise aloneness only to emerge and then throw oneself into all kinds of things. On the contrary, one should remain in this place of aloneness and not lose oneself in all kinds of actions, thoughts and feelings.

'How do you pass the time when work is done?' asked Tokuzan.
'I listen to the crickets and to rain. The moon is sometimes beautiful.'

The woman is alone with the vegetables that she grows, and when she has finished her work, she listens to the crickets and the rain. And the moon is sometimes beautiful. Just like that!

> After a pause, she continued, 'May I beg that you will instruct me in Buddhism?' A feeling of affinity made Tokuzan hold his tongue. The woman waited.

The feeling of affinity is something very important. This affinity functions according to set patterns on different levels of existence. There is affinity in the world of thoughts among like-minded people; there is also physical and spiritual affinity. But not just in the human world, there is also affinity in the animal and plant worlds. Even in the inorganic world one can observe affinities. From a Buddhist point of view it is part of the Dharma or the Tao.

> Then Tokuzan said, 'A man does not teach his equals. Rather you tell me.'

When two people meet they usually silently compare themselves and ask themselves whether they are equal to one another or not. Then they begin an exchange of views that leads to a certain confrontation. They lecture one another. But here it is very different: 'A person does not teach his equals.' In Japan and in ancient China and India this equality is silently acknowledged by bowing to one another.

> Aged wrinkles deepened as the woman smiled. 'I have nothing to tell,' she replied, 'and how should I begin?'
> 'Pray proceed,' said Tokuzan. The woman again made obeisance, but still had no word.
> 'In my monastery,' said Tokuzan, 'five hundred monks call

me Master, yet I know nothing and tell them nothing, for there is nothing, absolutely nothing. Were it not better to live in solitude and listen to crickets and rain?'

This 'There is nothing, absolutely nothing' is especially emphasised in Zen. This great Nothing, *sunyata* or *nirodha*, is what Joshu expressed with his *Mu*. People are very afraid of this great nothing. But plants and animals don't shy away from it, they simply exist in and through this nothing. They have no difficulty with it, admittedly they don't really know anything about it. They know just as little about it as a fish knows about water.

'Were it not better to live in solitude and listen to crickets and to rain?' As I said earlier, through an awareness of nature it is possible to move away a little from ones encapsulated 'I'. But nature doesn't consist only of individual forms like crickets, squirrels and grasses, etc., but also of what we might call *great nature*. The old woman said, 'The moon is sometimes beautiful.' That is an allusion to *great nature*. The rain too is an expression of great nature, coming as it does from the vast, infinite heavens.

The woman answered shyly, 'I tend vegetables, but hold no converse with them. But without me they would never nourish the villagers, and in time they would become weeds.'

Nowadays one has observed the interesting phenomenon that plants that are spoken to and lovingly tended thrive much better than those that are not spoken to. However, the old woman did not speak to the vegetables, but: 'Without me they would never nourish the villagers, and in time they would become weeds.' She put the emphasis on the act of service. One could argue that it was just a trade exchange because she cultivated and sold vegetables in order to be able to buy rice for herself. What matters here is that on the part of the old woman there is no desire to hold on, that is, she doesn't appropriate the plants. Have you ever observed how one can take over another person through verbal communication? One has to be very careful with these kinds of exchanges. It can happen quite easily that we mutually take possession of one another; and that naturally doesn't lead to liberation, quite the contrary. 'I tend vegetables, but hold no converse with them. But without me they would never nourish the villagers, and in time they would become weeds.' This activity is not taking for oneself, it is giving. It is a gesture of service.

> Tokuzan bowed to the woman. 'Well said, indeed. I return to my cabbages.' Departing, he reflected, 'Easier it is for a man to give birth to his own mother, than for the mind to achieve Every-Minute Zen.'

As I have already mentioned, this aloneness is based on a certain inner collectedness, however, not on an I-centredness. A great strength is required to remain collected in this great aloneness every single minute, constantly. It is very difficult for our heart/mind to achieve this Every-Minute Zen.

Let's take Judo or Karate as an example. When one enters the dojo for training, one has to leave oneself behind as well as everything that is happening outside on the street. One mustn't bring one's everyday self into the dojo or one will get injured or something else might happen. In order to do this combat justice, or more precisely, in order to become one with judo or karate, one has to be in a totally different state from that of one's everyday self. When after two to three hours one returns to the streets outside, one should retain the Judo or Karate. The same applies to the practice of Zen in the zendo. There one should experience Zen as an actuality, not just as an idea.

Then when the sitting is over, one returns to the outside world to be among people. They haven't got a clue about Zen and probably aren't interested anyway. There one is a person among many and looks like everyone else; one has taken off one's robe and doesn't strut around shouting, 'I'm a Zen-person, look at me!' Outwardly one is like everyone else, but more importantly, inwardly one continues sitting. This zazen is located inside. Zen is not in the buttocks on which one sits, though admittedly one can't sit without it. Therefore, Every-Minute-Zen is an awareness in which inside and outside are one.

So, what's with these two little woodblocks here on the table? I see them. There is nothing to be heard. There is only the contact of the eyes with the wood and the awareness thereof. Then I touch the woodblocks and feel their hard surface. Now there is the contact with the hand and the awareness of that contact. Now I pick them up with the hands in a special way and clap them against one another. Through this movement a sound arises in my ears. In the opposite direction it goes from the inside to the outside: consciousness, sense of hearing and the wooden blocks that produce a sound. Both directions are one, the entire happening is one procedure. Inside and outside are one; I'm not saying that they are *becoming* one, but that they *are* one. That is only a small example of Every-Minute-Zen, of the awareness of what is taking place in reality.

Bodhidharma showed what is most essential by saying nothing. He simply sat down in front of a bare cliff face and stared at it. He is portrayed with enormous bulging eyes. He didn't shift or move at all. He became one with the bare wall on which nothing was written; no ideas, no thoughts, no notions, just that. He did *samjana* with the cliff face. He showed that his spirit (Geist) and the cliff face were one. His spirit was emptied. Through this emptying one can be receptive to reality. If the spirit is not emptied, one is left with just a broth in which everything possible swims around and into which one constantly dips one's spoon and fishes something out. Important is to understand the matter at hand and then to put it into action. Tokuzan said to the old woman, 'Well said, indeed.' This 'in-deed' is a good word. In Zen too it depends on actualising something, putting it 'in-deed'.

THE RAISED PALM

Today I am going to read the entire story first and then give my commentary to specific parts of the story. This is actually the traditional Chinese way of giving commentaries.

'Why – ?' began Wu, but Tokuzan held up his hand.

'What – ?' he began again, but again met the raised palm. He remained silent. 'Well?' said the Master.

Wu raised his hand, and Tokuzan struck it down.

Mortified, the monk retired to meditate. He reasoned to himself; then, 'No,' said he, 'reasoning is not the way.' He would let go and dismiss the matter from his mind; then, 'No,' said he, 'Not that, not that.' Then what –? but the raised palm of the Master appeared before his closed eyes.

He opened his eyes and saw a new world. All the familiar objects were present, but all were cleansed from defilement of whatever sort. Before him stood a fir tree with a pigeon on a branch, and tree and bird were as hand and foot. Marvelling, he rose and strolled, and the world strolled with him, arm in arm, as a man and a girl in love.

He walked, yet not he, but his limbs moved. Grasses whispered to him, they echoed with ecstasy his inmost aspirations. So time passed, and the new world faded and gave place to the old.

He sought out Tokuzan, who was fanning himself on the porch. 'Well?' said the Master.

'I'm obliged at your great kindness,' said the monk.

'What have you gained?' asked Tokuzan.

The monk held up his hand.

'This fool can only imitate what others do,' said Tokuzan.

Wu struck down his own hand, bowed and retired.

Left alone, the Master said, 'I am obliged at your great kindness.' Then he went to bed.

This story also contains a kind of *mondo*, a spiritual encounter between disciple and master. As I have already mentioned, from such questions and answers koans later developed, which were used as methods for spiritual development.

When one hears such Zen stories, they may strike one as far-fetched nonsense. Or one may search for a deep hidden esoteric meaning behind the words, and then try and formulate something similar. Much has already been written and published about Zen and Zen anecdotes. Much of it also seems like real gold, but is forged. Some of it is forged so well that only an expert can assess it. But a real Zen master can't be fooled by that kind of Zen.

What is this raised hand all about? In a new-born child the windowpanes of the eyes are still completely clear, there are no impurities stuck to them, the consciousness is not yet distorted. In the eyes of this small child one can see the marvelling clarity, *myo*. The world has not yet been grasped with words, things, identities. Jesus said, 'Unless you become like little children, you will never enter the kingdom of heaven.' Of course, the heaven that is meant here is not the heaven one goes to after death. Heaven is here. If one practises meditation correctly, one goes to heaven, that is, to a clear realm of 'no-thing-ness'.

One day this little child with those clear eyes and unblemished spirit sees its hand for the first time. It doesn't know that it is its own hand. It smiles at it. It doesn't know the word 'hand', it knows nothing about 'my' hand or 'your' hand, it simply sees something that is suddenly there. It looks at this appearance and smiles. Then the hand falls down – for the baby doesn't yet have any control over its movements – the hand disappears as it appeared. Now the child cries. What appears, disappears again.

'Why?' began Wu. One is constantly asking, 'Why?' and when one asks 'why?', then one has to say 'because!' Aleister Crowley, who was often taken for a magician but was a great teacher, used to say, 'Curses upon you with your damned why.' 'Why do I exist? Why does the world exist? Why do I meditate? Why, why….?'

Due to this kind of thinking we are bound to the chain of cause and effect. Every cause has an effect, and every effect becomes the cause for the next effect. This chain is called the chain of dependent origination. According to the Buddha's teaching one has to liberate oneself from this chain. The great Vedanta teacher, Vivekananda, said, 'Human beings are bound by an iron chain – the chain of causality – and they have to exchange it for a for a golden chain – the chain of the Dharma, and then they have to get rid of this chain too.' First one is bound by the illusory aspects of human existence referred to as *maya*, and is liberated through discipline. Only a truly enlightened person can deliver such an allegory of the chain. This is not one of the intellectual falsifications I mentioned earlier. Only a really enlightened person can say that one then has to free oneself even from the true teaching of the chain of origination. Real meditation – whether it is Zen meditation or a form of Raja-yoga, or Christian mysticism or Sufi meditation – ultimately aims at liberation from both chains. But before one can completely liberate oneself one has to exchange the iron chain with the golden one. Meditation is an essential part of liberation, for the windowpanes of our eyes are no longer as clear and transparent as those of small children. In later life dust and flyspeck in the form of thoughts, wishes and desires is superimposed on them. One has to constantly clean these windows. Meditation is the cleansing of the windows, through which one looks at the world, and in which the world is mirrored. If the panes are clear, the seeing is clear. If a mirror is full of small specks, one gets a fright when looking into it, for one thinks the blemishes are on one's own face. There are many such examples.

If one asks 'why', one has to respond 'because!'. But Tokuzan held up his hand. There is a *non sequitur,* that is, a pun that makes no sense, but nonetheless is quite useful: 'Why is there a cow? – Because a vest has no sleeves.' A cow is, because it is there. No, God created it so that the milk industry could sell a lot of milk. That is why one has to convince people that they really need to drink a lot of milk, although nature only produces milk for babies. The little calf drinks milk, and the human mother has milk for her child. But if one wants to earn money with milk, then one has to persuade people that milk is good for their health and should be consumed all the time. And then one has to breed cows so that they give a lot of milk. Such nonsense exists in the world. Why?

One could also ask, 'Why are you?' 'Because mum and dad did something and then I was born.' 'And why did mum and dad do that?' 'Because they wanted me.' Or, 'No, they didn't want me at all, that was an accident, they wanted something else.' Or, 'God created me so that I could be grateful to him for bringing me into this valley of joy and sorrow.' People have so many ideas when they start with 'Why'.

Tokuzan raised his hand as if he wanted to shout, 'Stop!'

'What...?' Wu started to say. But Tokuzan didn't give him a chance to say anything, his raised hand immediately interrupted him. 'Wu' is actually quite an interesting name. In Chinese it means 'no'. But this Mr. No wants to know all kinds of things. He is searching for 'Yes' and 'Because'. But finally, he keeps quiet.

'Well?' said the Master. Wu raised his hand, and Tokuzan struck it down. – One doesn't actually know whether Wu had understood something just because he made the same gesture as Tokuzan. Anyway,

Tokuzan struck the hand down. There is a very famous story about Gutei. He was the Master of 'One-Finger-Zen'. In reply to every question put to him, Gutei held up his index finger. What is truth? What is Zen? What is samadhi? What is karma? What is rebirth? To all of these questions, he simply raised his index finger. This famous master had a disciple. There were quite a few people in the village who thought they might be able to get an answer to their questions from the disciple. But the disciple did exactly the same as the master and to every question he simply replied with a raised finger. Upon hearing about this, Gutei sent for his pupil. Gutei raised his finger and the monk out of habit raised his too, whereupon Gutei grabbed the pupil's finger and cut it off. The pupil screamed in pain and ran out of the room. Just before he reached the door, Gutei called his name and as the pupil turned around Gutei raised his finger. The pupil wanted to do the same, but – oh! In that moment the pupil was enlightened. Admittedly it cost him a finger, but that is a small loss in comparison to the gain of enlightenment.

After all he still had four fingers on that hand.

After Tokuzan struck down Wu's hand, Wu humbly withdrew. This was a prudent reaction, for he could have protested or complained. But his reaction was not egotistic. 'He reasoned with himself, and then he said, "No, reasoning is not the way."' – This we know about from our practice of meditation. One has to stop thinking. One has to avoid modifying consciousness as Patanjali said. One has to avoid being led astray by all kinds of thoughts, sensations and emotions.

'He would let go, and dismiss the matter from his mind; but then he thought, "No, not this, not that."' – Neither thinking nor not thinking, as it was already expressed in India even before the Buddha's time in the Advaita Vedanta teaching: *neti, neti* – not this, not that. One rejects everything. But then what? That cannot be explained, it can only be understood by doing it.

'The raised palm of the Master appeared before his closed eyes. He opened his eyes and saw a new world.' – Now his eyes were as clear as cleaned windowpanes. This experience was also expressed in the words of a Christian mystic: 'A new earth, a new heaven.' This is not the result of an artificially induced state as with all kinds of psychedelic drugs, but a pure, absolute primal state of consciousness. Through this clear consciousness, Wu saw a new world. He saw the phenomenal world in a new light. It was illuminated.

We only see things because light falls on them and is reflected back by them. The seeing in which everything appears as transparent in another light is referred to in Buddhism as the seeing of Nirmanakaya Buddha. That is, one sees the Buddha's body in its living multiplicity. The phenomenal world is the Buddha's *nirmanakaya*. 'All the familiar objects were present, but all were cleansed from defilement of whatever sort.' – Expressed in psychological terms, Wu, in this state, did not project anything of himself onto things, he saw them as they are. 'Before him stood a fir tree with a pigeon on a branch, and tree and bird were as hand and foot.' – Hand and foot belong together. Wu was experiencing unity.

'Marvelling, he rose and strolled, and the world strolled with him, arm in arm, as a man and a girl in love.' – This marvelling is the marvelling I mentioned earlier, myo. It is not an intellectual apprehension, it is the awesome beholding of reality. 'He walked, yet not he, but his limbs moved.' One should put the word 'his' limbs in quotation marks. The body as such has no I. In Soto Zen monks often sit with the single koan: 'This actual body is Buddha.' However, let it be understood that this *actual* body is not what I see here and regard as 'my' body. One has to understand what is meant by 'actual'. The raised hand of Tokuzan was an 'actual' hand. From where did this hand in its actuality originate? Where was this body before it emerged? Where was the oak before it became an oak? It was in the acorn. What is this state before coming into manifestation? The visible emerges from the invisible. Therefore, there is also a visible and an invisible body. The invisible body from which everything emerges is called the *dharmakaya* in Buddhism.

So, Wu didn't walk himself, his limbs moved. 'Grasses whispered to him, they echoed with ecstasy his innermost aspirations.' – This innermost yearning of all humans, whether they are aware of it or not, is the wish to reach the state of unity. They want to be liberated from the confrontational state of duality. The Vedanta teaches of the reconciliation of opposites. Opposites need not be hostile, they can be reconciled. In love, a man and a woman do not oppose one another, they are reconciled in a state of unity; and though he is still a man and she still a woman, there is no self-assertiveness with emphasis on superiority or inferiority based on gender differences. In love dualism is reconciled, even the dualism that one carries within oneself. Nowadays depth psychology concerns itself with the dualism in the human being, though two thousand years ago in India and China this was already understood. One has to come to this unity within oneself. That is why someone who has found themselves, has sorted themselves out, is referred to as a hermaphrodite. They have unified Hermes, wisdom, and Aphrodite, love, within themselves. In this story too, it is said, '…and the world strolled with him, arm in arm, like a man and a girl in love.' Our deepest yearning is therefore to reach the state of unity; whether one experiences this as unity with God or as samadhi or as a mystical marriage, the actuality is the same. The basic experience is the same for everyone, regardless of whether they are Indian, Chinese or European – in the depths of their being, they all yearn to be united with what is truly real.

'So time passed, and the new world faded and gave place to the old.' And this is something one also experiences. One steps into samadhi, and then one comes out again. The new world faded. The perfume evaporates. The meditative state moves into the background and makes room for the old. Everyone who meditates will experience this. But if one is deeply rooted in meditation, then this is no longer the case. Admittedly, one goes around in the world, does this and that, feels this and that, thinks this and that, experiences this and that, remembers this and that, lives in space and time, yet inwardly one remains in samadhi. One uses one's head, one uses one's hands and feet, arms and legs, but one remains in samadhi. Jesus said, 'Abide in me' – the Logos. It all depends on the abiding. The same thing is stated in the *Bhagavad Gita*, real liberation comes through abiding, also the getting rid of the golden chain. This is where Wu got to.

'He sought out Tokuzan, who was fanning himself on the porch. "Well?" said the Master.' – At their last encounter the Master had also said, 'Well?'

'I am obliged at your great kindness,' said the monk. – what was his great kindness? The raised hand and the striking down of Wu's raised hand. For thereby Wu came to his insight. He discovered: 'Neither this, nor that', neither thinking, nor not-thinking. That is true meditation. There are also forms of meditation that are not genuine, that don't possess any real validity.

'What have you gained?' asked Tokuzan. – In order to gain, one has to lose. That is a principle of life. Every gain involves a loss. Jesus once said, 'For what shall it profit a man, if he shall gain the whole world, and lose his own soul?'

'The monk held up his hand.' – Now this gesture was genuine. Whereupon Tokuzan said, 'This fool can only imitate what others do.' – That is characteristic of Zen, for there are two types of fool: there are stupid fools and there are wise fools. The Sufis understand this concept very well. For Tokuzan to say, 'This fool can only imitate others,' is a splendid compliment. Previously Wu had really only imitated and so Tokuzan struck the hand down. If one superficially compliments a person in Zen in order to flatter their ego, this is considered mean. On the other hand, if one shouts at a student, 'You worthless idiot, you despicable wretch!' then the student is really worth something. If you hand me a piece of lead to make a sword, I can try for a long time. Can you hold lead in a fire? It melts and is suddenly no longer there. Give me a piece of iron! That I can forge by holding it in fire and water and beating it until it has the right purity and hardness so it can be honed. That is the alchemy of the sword. That is why one speaks of the Sword of Wisdom.

When a master yells at his student, 'You're a worthless imbecile, pull yourself together', then he is really worth something, but he has to recognise his own intrinsic worth. Wu understood, 'He struck down his own hand, bowed and retired. Left alone, the Master said, "I am obliged at your great kindness."' – Tokuzan and Wu were one. No difference. Then Tokuzan went to bed.

In essence all humans are one. But what is usually emphasised? *My* personality. This is how I am, and I can't get on with you because you are different, etc. That is our magnificent individualism! But if individualism rests on the foundation of unity, then it is something completely different. Yes! – differentiation at the basis of unity. However, differentiation that is not rooted in unity only leads to conflict; conflict with oneself and conflict in relation to the outside world.

THE OTHER MONK

A monk asked Tokuzan, 'What is the fundamental principle of Buddhism?'

That is a good and valid question. There are many possible answers to that. Every school or sect of Buddhism would answer it slightly differently. Tokuzan'a answer corresponds to the Zen School.

Tokuzan said, 'You must ask the other monk.'
From time to time the monk repeated his question and always he received the same answer. Finally, he ceased to ask, but the problem never passed from his mind.

Tokuzan gave this questioning monk a koan: 'You must ask the other monk.' Though with time the monk stopped asking the question because he always received the same answer, he nonetheless always carried the question around with him. What is the fundamental principle of Buddhism? Ask the other monk! Who is the other monk?

One day, while absorbed in meditation, he was disturbed by a kitten at play. Efforts to regain the lost state of absorption were futile and he found his anger mounting.

Was he cross with himself, was he annoyed by the harmless playing kitten? Really he should have been angry with himself, why did he allow himself to be disturbed in his meditation?

He sought to meditate on the virtues of tolerance and compassion, but all without avail. Whereupon he said to himself, 'Let it be the other monk's concern,' and he played with the kitten.

That was very reasonable. As he was meditating on tolerance and compassion, why shouldn't he be tolerant with himself and even have compassion for himself for allowing himself to be disturbed like that. Now he played with the kitten and this play became his meditation. 'Let it be the other monk's concern.'

> Slowly thereafter the habit grew of leaving all concerns,
> both mystical and mundane, to the other monk. He ate
> and slept and worked when he would, with the big stick of
> Tokuzan on occasion to fashion his inclinations.

It is important for us to understand what the stick in Tokuzan's hand means. It is not for punishment. The use of the stick is often misunderstood. In Tokuzan's hand the stick is an extension of his spiritual function. The blow with the stick means: 'Wake up! Stop dreaming! Become aware of yourself!' Becoming aware of oneself is not to be confused with one's own emotions and sensations. One should become aware of the pure, naked, true self, without the apparel of any thoughts, emotions or sensations. For this purpose, the stick is used in the Zen School. Sometimes the teacher also resorts to a shout. That too means 'Wake up!' This shout goes back to Rinzai and to his teacher Obaku.

The expression used here – 'to fashion the inclinations' – is perhaps a little difficult to understand, so I will try and clarify it somewhat. First of all, it is a matter of really understanding this actual, true self. But this self doesn't exist in a vacuum. It is, so to say, embodied. There is the body, and there are the sense organs, thoughts and other contents of consciousness. The unconscious contents are the tendencies. The Buddha analysed human consciousness and accordingly distinguished five *skandhas*, that is, 'layers'. He described the basic, innermost layer as the fundamental consciousness. In this fundamental consciousness there are tendencies. It is sometimes somewhat difficult to find a fitting translation for Sanskrit terms. The tendencies are the directional movements of consciousness. The next layers form the thought patterns, the sensory impressions and the body in contact with the so-called objective world. Using the hand as an example, one could say that the thumb is the fundamental consciousness. The fundamental consciousness on its own cannot do much. What can I achieve with the thumb alone? The tendencies would be comparable with the index finger. Consciousness is given expression through the tendencies. Whether it is described as heredity or karma, is immaterial. For example, there is the tendency of consciousness to direct itself outwards, but there is also the tendency to direct oneself inwards. Thumb and index finger together can already achieve something, but on its own the index finger can't do anything. But for the hand to be able to perform all its functions, it needs all five fingers. Fundamental consciousness is closely connected with the body, the senses, the thoughts and the tendencies, whereby the tendencies determine the direction or inclination of the other functions. This can be observed in everyone. In a sense these inclinations must be formed and fashioned.

In the East they were already looking into the nature of human consciousness over many thousands of years ago, whereas here in the West research was focused more on the external world. In the meantime, psychology with its many schools of thought has also developed here in the West. But in comparison with Eastern psychology, Western psychology is still in its infancy. Eastern philosophy goes much deeper and accordingly also leads to a deeper understanding. In the West we are still treating symptoms; we don't come close to the real cause. I know this from personal experience from the time of my medical and psychiatric practice.

Here in this little story, when it is said that Tokuzan's big stick fashioned the monk's inclinations, it is more about the essence of consciousness. In Zen people are sometimes compared to trees. They have deep roots which stabilise and nourish them. They have a trunk out of which the branches, twigs and leaves grow. The branches, twigs and leaves which spread outwards are comparable to the senses with their consequent thoughts, feelings and sensations. As a rule, this human tree doesn't stand upright, but usually inclines in one or the other direction. The human body itself does stand up straight, but the human spirit is still not able to do so – it doesn't strive from the earth straight up to heaven, but pursues one or more tendencies.

In Zen training the tree is now pulled in the opposite direction. If for example it leans to the right, it must be pulled to the left. After a certain time, it can be released and it will stand upright. This principle can be clearly observed in Japanese gardens. There entire trees or branches are bound up tightly until they grow straight, or as it seems straight to the Japanese eye. The emphasis of tying the human tree up in the opposite direction of its tendencies, originates from the Japanese form of Zen. Though this was not practised in China, there too it was deemed necessary to recognise the tendencies and fashion them. Sometimes a person experiences internal conflicts because various inclinations pull in different directions. Often they don't even realise that they house such tendencies and that these are the cause of their conflicts, which in turn are the cause for the difficulties within themselves and with the world around them. In most cases our psychology tries to treat the difficulties by proceeding to the level of the conflict. It seldom focusses on the tendencies, on the crux of the matter. Also in bringing up children these inclinations should be fashioned. This task is undertaken by Tokuzan and his big stick. The story continues:

After many years the Master said to test him, 'What is the fundamental principle of Buddhism?'

'That is indeed a question to engage the attention,' agreed the monk.

He didn't give an answer, he just agreed that it was an important question. Naturally there are many questions that engage the attention – philosophical questions, religious questions, scientific question, questions that concern art, ecology, politics, economics, etc.

'I asked you, what is the fundamental principle? said Tokuzan.

'I replied, the problem is well put,' said the monk.

Here we have the spiritual Judo which I mentioned previously. Nowadays this almost no longer happens. With my teacher Sokei-an, the opportunity occasionally arose for that kind of spiritual combat.

'Answer my question,' shouted the Master. '
Ask the other monk,' was screamed back in his face.

So, who is the other monk? There is a famous koan which I would like to mention in this context: A master invited another master to tea. The large window that led into the garden was covered with a blind as the sun had earlier shone too brightly into the room. But now it was slowly growing dark. The master called for two monks to come in and roll up the blind. Together both monks evenly rolled up the blind and then left the room. As they were leaving the master said to his guest, 'One monk won, the other monk lost.' Who is the other monk?

When students are given a koan, they work with it by observing it. One shouldn't say a koan is 'answered'. It is not about answering, rather about observing the koan until one sees what it says. When one suddenly correctly sees through this quandary, namely the question, it is as if it has disappeared. Where there was a barrier before, now there is nothing. That is why one speaks of 'striding- or passing through' a koan, as if one were passing through a barrier.

If one wanted to approach the question of the other monk psychologically from the perspective of our Western thinking, one could say: A human being is divided, being at the same time both his own subject and object. I am myself, but at the same time I can observe myself, and my thoughts, my body and my reactions, etc. Who is it then who says, 'I have such and such thoughts, feelings and wishes.'? Who is it, who observes in this way? And who is it, who is being observed?

As I have mentioned before, in the earliest school of Buddhism, in the Theravada, there is a meditation practice called Vipassana, in which one sits and observes everything that arises – thoughts, sense impressions, memories, physical sensations, and so on. It is like stepping back inwardly and just observing. One doesn't criticise or evaluate, but just looks on like when watching a film. Through this meditation one identifies less with the unfolding scene and relates more objectively to oneself. Only after one is objective with regard to oneself, can one be objective about others and the world. It is wrong to expect objectivity from others when one can't be objective about oneself. Who is the other monk?

The monk in our story slowly left all his concerns, whether of a mystical or mundane nature, to the other monk, while he himself ate, slept and worked as he wished, and Tokuzan shaped his inclinations with the big stick. And in this way, he recognised the other monk in himself.

Outwardly there is a monk, he wears a robe, eats, sleeps, works and plays with a cat. It is as simple as that. And then there is the other monk. What is the fundamental principle of Buddhism? When ordinary people want to answer this question, they can proceed philosophically, theologically or in some scientific way or other. But the real answer will not be found in this way. Ordinary people cannot answer this question. All these teachers who set themselves up and explain Buddhism on the basis of the scriptures, expound the fundamental principle of Buddhism according to their school with many words. Yet the fundamental principle is what the Buddha called nirvana. For ordinary people nirvana is impossible to attain. In their comings and goings, they can only live according to the dictates of their tendencies. The only one who can attain nirvana is the other monk. Tell me right at this very moment of your existence who the other monk is. What is his name? If you deliberate over this, you can't see him.

In the Christian religion one receives a given name, and with it one is baptised in the name of the Father, the Son and the Holy Ghost. Nowadays this has all become very superficial, but in former times the baptismal name was very important. Even in ancient Egypt there was a name one received from a priest. This name was known only to the person and the priest. It was the true name, not the name given one by one's father and mother. In Hinduism as well as in Buddhism, one is also given a religious name when one joins an ashram or a temple. In the past, it was customary for the novice who wished to enter a Zen temple to be asked for his name. If he answered with his family name, it could happen that he would not be allowed to enter. The name one gets from one's family is not the right name. One has to find one's true name. Not until one knows who one truly is, can one answer the question of the name correctly, so that the teacher sees that this is someone who can be admitted and whose tendencies can be fashioned with the stick.

As you know, it is not possible to forge a sword out of lead. Therefore one shouldn't approach a Zen master like a clump of lead. One should at least be like iron, if not like steel. Expressed astrologically: not Saturn but Mars. Mars is the planet of fighting, and iron is attributed to Mars. Zen training is a battle, namely a battle with oneself. In order to realise the true self, one has to do battle with the personal self.

In the New Testament there is a passage where Jesus asks Simon, 'Who am I?' To which Simon replies, 'You are the Christ.' Jesus then asks a second time, 'Who am I?' 'You are the Christ.' He asked for the third time, 'Who am I?' And again the answer is, 'You are the Christ.' Thereupon Jesus said, 'Simon, you are Peter and on this rock I will build my church.' And then he continued, 'But this night before the rooster crows three times, you will deny knowing me three times.' And so it came to pass. On the one hand, Simon, who later became Peter, was a weak man, but within him lived a colossal strength, that had yet to emerge. That was the inner tendency, the inner nature of this fisherman called Simon. The weak person with the enormous inherent strength. From a Zen perspective this is well known. One should recognise this Peter, with all his human weaknesses and human fallibility, in oneself. Expressed in the Christian sense it is that which is created in the image of God, the spirit of God in us. In the Old Testament it is said that God breathed his own breath into the clay form of Adam. With that he gave him a *ruach*, that, is a living soul.

Who is the other monk? Recognise him in yourself. This can be done through correct meditation, but at the same time one carries on with what one has to do in daily life. In all one's activities one should not forget the other monk, for it is he who can answer the fundamental questions of existence. One of these questions is: Who am I really? What is my real name?

We live in the world of names and forms, *namarupadhatu*. But there is another world that goes beyond the world of forms and names. One could also call it the nameless world. What would be the name of this nameless world? That is very paradoxical: the name of the nameless world! One must pass from the world of forms and names through to the nameless and formless world. That is why in Zen one chants the *Prajnaparamita Sutra*, in which one continuously repeats: the world of forms and the formless world are one. How can one really understand that the world of names and forms and the nameless and formless world are one? And in order to gain an understanding of this, not just philosophically, but concretely, the tool of the koan was devised in China.

Tokuzan received the news that his friend and fellow-master Huang Tzu had retired from active work. It appeared that he had made over the monastery at which he had presided to his former head monk, and he himself was living in seclusion in the hills.

Tokuzan was unconvinced that all was well. He decided to visit Huang Tzu, and one day he arrived at the hermitage. Barking dogs greeted him with mocked ferocity. He found Huang Tzu busy preparing a meal. The visitor was made welcome and soon rice was served. After they had eaten, Tokuzan broached the subject of his visit.

'I hear you have retired from teaching.'

Huang had been in a merry mood. Now his brow darkened. He said, 'I am an old man, but I am no longer a vicious old man.'

Tokuzan looked his amazement. Huang picked up a pebble and threw it for the dogs to chase. He reflected for a moment and then recited:

> 'I watch the little dogs,
> How assiduously they seek to influence others,
> Force them into line,
> Scratch, bite, anything to attain their ends.
> I watch the feverish activity;
> As seed is sown in wanton waste
> And unashamed abandon.
> So once I taught, argued, coerced
> With fierce joy and subsequent disappointment.
> Now I watch the dogs and think,

There go the teachers and preachers,
Who know not what they do but call it good.
I call it masturbation.'

Tokuzan nodded his comprehension. He said, 'There was a time when I too thought the same. An old woman who cultivated cabbage pointed out my error. Her logic was as clear as muddy water but her conclusion was correct. Hence I still teach and preach.'

The Masters regarded one another. Opinions differed. Opinions will always differ.

Huang said, 'That is you opinion. I see it as a small stone chased by a little dog,'

Tokuzan said, 'In truth your opinion is the little dog that chases the small stone.'

The Masters laughed. They differed, but they always would agree.

Tokuzan rose to depart. He observed, 'I return to my indulgence.'

Huang rose to bid him farewell. He responded, 'I have enjoyed listening to your sermon.'

Both men spoke their minds.

That is a very nice story. Nice? ... Malice turns to kindness, kindness becomes malice. Human beings are caught in this kind of a delusion; it seems to be very difficult to find a way out of this labyrinth of good and evil.

'"I hear you have retired from teaching." Huang had been in a merry mood. Now his brow darkened.' – as if he were saying, 'Why do you have to start with that? I have retired. You do your own thing, I do my own thing. What do you want from me?'

But, 'He said, "I am an old man, but I am no longer a vicious old man."' – that is, in the monastery he was a vicious man, now he is no longer vicious. 'Tokuzan looked his amazement,' – one shows one's amazement by raising one's eyebrows.

'Huang picked up a pebble and threw it for the dogs to chase. He reflected for a moment and then recited: "I watch the little dogs, how assiduously they seek to influence others, force them into line, scratch, bite, anything to attain their ends...."' – that's just how little dogs are, isn't it? But we are not little dogs, we are human and on no account do we behave like that!

There was once a very good teacher, I even met him personally. He was very controversial, but I regard him as a very great teacher. I am referring here to Gurdjieff. He used to say, 'He who lives like a dog, will also die like a dog.' In other words, if you don't realise your true self, you are like a dog and will perish like a dog. The dog can have several different meanings. For instance, there is the 'Hound of Heaven' who pursues one constantly, is hard on one's heels and from whom one runs away. In Zen there is Master Joshu's famous question, 'Does a dog have Buddha-nature?' It is said that all sentient beings have Buddha-nature, and a dog is a sentient being. Yet Joshu answers with the famous 'Mu', 'No'. And there are various other meanings associated with the dog. Huang said, 'I watch the little dogs, how assiduously they seek to influence others, force them into line, scratch, bite, anything to attain their ends.' – One should stop acting like these little dogs. Or does one not recognise oneself in this picture?

'I watch the feverish activity; as seed is sown in wanton waste and unashamed abandon.' – There is a passage in the New Testament where it says, 'Do not give what is holy to the dogs; nor cast your pearls before swine.' – I won't give you the pearl of wisdom because you are a dog. I only give you lies, because you are a liar yourself. I will serve you lies until you recognise the truth through the lie. Then you can be grateful to the lie because it led you to the truth. Perhaps it can be understood like this.

'So once I taught, argued, coerced with fierce joy and subsequent disappointment.' – This too has a familiar ring to it. 'Now I watch the dogs and think, there go the teachers and preachers, who know not what they do but call it good. I call it masturbation.' – Yes, there is something like spiritual self-gratification, too.

'Tokuzan nodded his comprehension. He said, "There was a time when I too thought the same. An old woman who cultivated cabbage pointed out my error."' – In other words, a very simple woman. She wasn't a teacher. She didn't preach or instruct, she just cultivated cabbage. She pointed out Tokuzan's error. One plants all kinds of seeds in the garden of consciousness and cultivates the burgeoning sprouts.

'Her logic was as clear as muddy water but her conclusion was correct.' – Why was her logic not as clear as pure spring water? One usually thinks that one can achieve clarity through logic, and logic is considered the discipline of thinking. But in reality, all these musings are just stirring around in muddy water, because it always revolves around human affairs. But the old woman's conclusion was correct. 'Hence I still teach and preach.'

Huang Tzu said that to teach and preach was a bad thing, but Tokuzan said that to teach and preach was a good thing. How can a bad thing be good, how can a good thing be bad? Is there an absolute bad or an absolute good? Can bad not be changed into good and vice versa? 'The Masters regarded one another. Opinions differed.' – My opinion, your opinion!

'Huang said, "That is your opinion. I see it as a small stone chased by a little dog." Tokuzan said, "In truth your opinion is the little dog that chases the small stone."' – Well, in all fairness it has to be said that this is a superb *mondo*. 'The Masters laughed. They differed, but they always would agree.'

The little stone chased by the dog; or the little dog who chases after the stone! This is an image that we should look at carefully. There is a koan concealed in there, and we ourselves are this koan.

'Tokuzan rose to depart. He observed, "I return to my indulgence."' – Which indulgence should one follow? One should become aware of these inclinations. I presume most of you remember playing with roly-poly dolls when you were children. They were hollow inside and contained a lead weight which caused the doll to return to an upright position regardless of how it was put down. Originally these dolls represented Bodhidharma, but later they became other characters as well. If one focusses on the *hara*, like Bodhidharma, then no matter what happens, one will always return to the equilibrium of the upright position. Whether one turns forwards or backward, right or left, all movements turn around the centre of gravity. The centre of gravity is motionless, leaning forwards, backwards, etc. is movement. In the *Tao-te-ching*, Lao-tzu says, 'Stillness is the ruler of movement.' The force of gravity always brings all movement back to the central place of rest. In Zen meditation all the strength is collected in the *hara*, and when one then moves again, *hara* is the master of movement. In the martial arts like Judo, Aikido, and Kung Fu, the most important thing is to retain this sense of gravity in the *hara*. From there, the yin-or yang-movements originate and merge into one another. I only mention this in passing, but it does have a connection to this story.

Huang Tzu also followed his inclination. He didn't voice it like Tokuzan, but it is obvious. First he was active, now he is passive. There is a fundamental controversy around the question of whether or not the attempt should be made to disseminate the so-called truth in all cases. Some say one should wait until the individual is ripe enough for it. Only then should one offer them the 'taste of the truth'. But who should be responsible for deciding whether the individual is ripe or not? Others say that the truth should be offered to everyone and what the individual makes of it is his own affair. One doctor might prescribe a diet for his patient's cure. Another doctor might say, 'Eat what you like, the body will naturally know what to do with it.'

People are offered Christianity, Hinduism, Buddhism or another teaching – in each case it is a prepared meal with a specific taste – and they are asked to eat it. This approach trusts that the spiritual stomach will know how to digest it. That is one point of view. The other insists that the individual must be ripe, before he is offered a specific dish. According to this view it is necessary to know what psychologically motivates the individual. Do they want the truth to make themselves great, to inflate themselves spiritually? Or do they want the truth to escape what they can't deal with? They can't get along with themselves, can't cope with others, can't get along in the world, and so they seek refuge in the so-called truth. Or do they want the truth for its own sake? One has to be clear about one's motivations If you have a neurosis, then free yourself of that neurosis. Whether you then still really want the truth will become clear. Because if you free yourself from that neurosis, you might be content, have a pleasant attitude towards life, and are then perhaps no longer interested in knowing the truth.

According to the other view, you should pursue the truth regardless of your motivation. Whether it is a neurotic need or a real desire to know the truth is immaterial, because when you have realised the truth, then everything that motivated you, whether neurosis, escape, compensation or whatever else, falls away. So even in regard to knowing the truth there are different opinions.

The question still remains: how did the old woman who cultivated cabbages convince Tokuzan not to give up when he too wished to withdraw from preaching? How, with her muddied logic but correct conclusion, did she persuade him to continue teaching even though teachers often are confronted by sneering and yapping dogs? There are not just tail-wagging little dogs who chase after stones, but also fierce barking dogs. One often has to wonder what it is that calls itself human.

In Zen special emphasis is put on the teaching of *sunya* or *sunyata*, which is sometimes also referred to as the great void. The following story of Tokuzan deals with this absolute fundamental principle.

The sister of So-So fell sick. A Taoist priest applied his texts, but the remedies were unavailing; the fever mounted and it seemed that she must die.

So-So was very sad. He came to Tokuzan, who told him, 'Darkness is but the absence of light, the false is but the shadow of the true. Truth is life and life is everlasting. See your sister well and strong and know that she will live.'

So-So did as directed and in a little while the girl was well. Then So-So felt he knew the truth and it made him glad indeed.

Later, a son of one of the villagers lay ill. When So-So heard the news he was convinced, he could cure the child. He approached the parents who welcomed him with gratitude and faith. The omens were propitious. Next day the boy was dead.

So-So was disconsolate, and the Master sought him out. He said, 'So-So, there is nothing true anywhere, but to seek for truth is good. Yet there is that which is better, and that is to know and love that nothing which is true.'

He left So-So alone, and the monk was alone in truth. He felt nothing belonged, there was no support; even old Hui-Neng had said, 'The true is nowhere to be found.'

No, there was nothing. Absolutely nothing. Only a monk in a quiet place who prized what he perceived.

Why was So-So's sister cured of her illness, while the son of the neighbour died? So-So experienced the healing of his sister, and believed that he now knew the truth and that made him happy. When Tokuzan told him, 'See your sister well and strong and know that she will live,' he directed his strength to his thinking, and in this case his strength was effective. But in the case of the boy, it didn't work. So-So regarded the power of thought as the truth itself. Then he had to experience that this power that he believed to be the truth was ineffective. Now he was disconsolate and Tokuzan sought him out. He said, 'So-So, there is nothing true anywhere, but to seek for truth is good.' We usually believe that what we consider to be true is in fact the expression of the truth. But that is obviously not the case. What we perceive in the phenomenal world are only the appearances of forms. In the esoteric Buddhist school of Asanga, it is taught that everything that one experiences, sees, hears, senses or thinks is only a representation. If I strike this gong, we hear a sound. If one is deaf, there is no sound. The vibrations are indeed there, but they don't translate into a sound because the ear doesn't react. Our ears only hear certain frequencies, not others. For example, there are dog whistles, which we can't hear, though dogs can. It is the same with regard to all manifestations, they are specific frequencies of vibrations which our sense organs perceive.

Tokuzan said, 'There is nothing true anywhere, but to seek for truth is good.' – If one concerns oneself with the theory of knowledge and investigates whether what one believes one knows is true knowledge or just a notion or an assumption, then this is a search for the truth. The epistemological differentiation between the world of appearances on the one hand and the on the other the noumenal world, from which the world of phenomena is abstracted, this is also a search for the truth.

So-So's thinking and its impact belong in the realm of appearances, they are phenomena. The power of thought does exist, but it is not the ultimate truth. It is not the noumenal. The same power did not work for the neighbour's son, although it was the same So-So who used it. In one case it worked, in the other not. Yet So-So thought he had found the truth in the power of thought. Then Tokuzan came and showed him what it really comes down to by saying that there is nothing true anywhere, but that one should still seek for the truth. So what is this truth that one should search for, even though nothing true exists? The answer is almost self-evident: that nothing true exists, is the truth. Therefore the theory of knowledge says that the perceived, which is not true as such, is the expression of the truth, of the noumenon. The epistemologists got as far as understanding this, but they said the noumenal itself is not knowable.

Zen Buddhism takes a final step further and teaches that the noumenal can also be realised. Not just the phenomenal world, but also the 'ultimate reality' out of which it emerges, is knowable. This is expressed in the *Prajnaparamita Sutra* as: Form is not different from no-form, no-form is not different from form. In other words, the world of appearances is reality, reality is the world of appearances. Or one can differentiate and speak of noumenal and phenomenal reality.

Every physicist would readily understand this. But that is a scientific and philosophical observation. As such it is true, but it is no more than a theoretical and philosophical observation. In India these kinds of reflections have been written down since eternity. But it was then stipulated that the theory had to be realised, that it shouldn't just remain a theory. And so the various schools of yoga and Buddhism developed.

In the Zen School this theme is approached in a very specific way. For instance, I strike this gong and explain that what emerges are vibrations, which are translated into a sound for our ears. But something else has to be present besides the vibration and the ear, and that is something that discerns the sound. A perceptiveness, more specifically consciousness has to be present. From this the question arises, 'What is it that sees this object we call a gong and hears its sound?' At that moment when the ear receives the sound and the consciousness perceives it, object, sound and perception have become one; theoretically they can be differentiated, but in reality they are one. In Zen meditation and in the yoga practice of *samjana* this oneness is realised. I see this object, and because I see where it is I can strike it and hear its sound. I am aware of it. If I close my eyes, I no longer see the object. If I concentrate fully on the sound, I can hear it even more clearly. After a while the sound disappears from the ear, but it carries on ringing in the consciousness. For the eye and the ear the appearance has vanished, yet it continues to resonate in the consciousness. Seeing and hearing, forms and sounds, as well as the thoughts and words in relation to our seeing and hearing, all belong in the world of phenomena. There is nothing true in them. But there is also nothing true outside of them. Hence, for us, everything that is present is an expression or evidence of this truth.

Tokuzan continued, 'Yet there is that which is better, and that is to know and love this nothing which is true.' – What is this nothing? In India 'emptiness', which is strongly emphasised in Zen, is represented as the god Sunya in heaven. He scatters white blossoms down to earth like snowflakes. The petals wilt very quickly. The impermanence of phenomena manifests emptiness. The state of emptiness is called *sunyata*. Some Zenists who wish to approach this nothing, enter the samadhi of nothing, *nirodha-samadhi*. This sinking into nothingness already existed in India and in Taoism too. In this samadhi one realises that all manifestations have their being in nothingness, just as the entire cosmos with all its worlds, stars and galaxies exists in the emptiness of space. If this emptiness did not exist, no phenomena would exist. Out of and within this nothingness everything exists.

This is the belief of a specific school of thought and meditation. But is this the samadhi of nothingness that Tokuzan is referring to when he says, 'Yet there is that which is better, and that is to know and love this nothing which is true.'? No, Tokuzan is not speaking of the samadhi of nothingness. He is talking about the realisation that nothing exists and that that is the truth. In Buddhist terms it is expressed as, 'All *dharmas* are empty', that is, all phenomena are empty.

Tokuzan showed So-So the two aspects of truth. First he said, 'Darkness is but the absence of light, the false is but the shadow of the true. Truth is life and life is everlasting.' Then he said, 'So-So, there is nothing true anywhere, but to seek for truth is good. Yet there is that which is better, and that is to know and love this nothing which is true.' – As I have already said, it is easy to dialectically say that the phenomenal world is the noumenal, and the noumenal is the phenomenal world. But that has to be translated into an actuality. And thus So-So came to a realisation that was not theoretical. First he thought he had realised the truth, but that was a mistake. But then when he was actually alone, 'he felt nothing belonged.' We know that not a thing exists without everything else. There is nothing, whether large or small, simple or complicated, no atom or molecule that could exist without everything else. Everything is interrelated. But now 'So-So felt that nothing belonged, there was no support; even old Hui Neng had said, "The true is nowhere to be found."' – So-So was unable to hold on to anything. In Zen this situation is described as 'letting go with both hands.' When you let go with both hands you fall into the underground of being, into the abyss. Let go and fall into this unfathomable nothing!

There was no support for So-So. 'No, there was nothing. Absolutely nothing. Only a monk in a quiet place who prized what he perceived.' – Who is it, or what is it that sees colours and forms because it has eyes, and hears sounds because it has ears that seem to function in a certain way? Who is it, or what is it that perceives? Who is this monk in a quiet place? Does one necessarily have to look for him in a monastery or an ashram or a Zen temple? The monk and the quiet place are within ourselves. The monk prizes what he perceives, and he knows that it is a world of appearances, and that this phenomenal world is the expression of reality. Through meditation one finds in oneself the monk in the quiet place who prizes what he perceives: people, things, everything. One should see this monk, not just in oneself, but in each person.

The monk and the quiet place do not belong to the world of phenomena, but the monk encounters this world of appearances and prizes it. At birth there is something that accompanies us into this world. For a while after birth it is still manifest, but then it is relinquished. Why is it left alone? Because one grows up, is subjected to conditions, develops into an adult with a personal identity. But something has remained behind and is all alone. The Sankya School uses the image of Purusha who has fallen into a state of oblivion. He has forgotten himself. We are not what we see when we look in the mirror; every one of us is the monk in the quiet place who prizes what he perceives: *tat tvam asi* – thou art that.

In Zen meditation one simply goes to this place where the monk is and focusses the attention. One shouldn't fall asleep or dream. One should be awake and prize what one perceives.

THE MONK WHO GOT DRUNK ON TEA

> Tokuzan was interviewing a new monk. 'What's your name?' he asked.
>
> 'Yesterday I got drunk on tea,' answered the monk, who thought he knew Zen.

Nowadays there are actually quite a few people who imagine that they know Zen. I have deliberately used the word 'imagine'. They have nosed around in Zen like one uses pigs to find truffles. They have heard something about it and have read everything possible, and implausible, about Zen and now feel that they know what Zen is. For instance, in the 60s there was a famous man who spoke and wrote really well about Zen. However, he presented the public with a false intellectual picture of Zen and the hippies made him into a guru. But even today there are intellectuals who profess to know Zen, but who have no practical understanding of it. From a Zen point of view, they are just silly intellectuals. Real Zen is very different. Just sitting zazen or listening to talks by Zen masters is not enough. If zazen doesn't lead to any insight, if it doesn't enlighten, it is worthless. One can sit and sit or practise this or that kind of meditation, but without insight it is just a waste of time. In that case one would be better off pursuing a sensible activity instead of just sitting around. In order to prevent blind sitting the koan was devised as tool. With the help of the koan one has to prove that one has a realisation. This tool, however, like all tools must be used properly for it to work effectively. Just sitting your body down is not Zen yet. One has to sit inwardly too and quieten down the mind. This samadhi should not be a blind samadhi.

There is a famous story from India which illustrates this point: A yogi sits in meditation by the roadside. A young man sees this and thinks, 'Here I have the opportunity to ask a wise man a question.'

And so he asked, 'Venerable Sir, would you please be so kind as to answer a question?' The yogi got very annoyed and said, 'How dare you disturb me in my meditation and pull me out of my samadhi. I am a sick man and I suffer: only when I am in samadhi am I free of my suffering. Go away and don't bother me!' In this meditation there is no insight, no enlightenment and hence no real liberation. It is just an escape. Equally useless is it to boast and say, 'I am going into samadhi.' That is just puffing oneself up, spiritual inflation. If you want to impress others there are better ways of demonstrating it.

So Tokuzan had a visit from a clever monk like that, who to the question of what he was called replied, 'Yesterday I got drunk on tea.' – He thought he knew Zen and could impress Tokuzan with that answer.

> 'I asked you, what is your name,' repeated the Master with patience.

Yes, he was patient. My teacher Sokei-an would not have been so patient and would probably have given the monk a slap.

> The monk was ashamed. 'My name is Sen T'sen,' he said.
> 'You are a clever fellow, Sen T'sen. Why come to me?' asked the Master.
> 'Please instruct me,' said Sen, with contrition.

That was a good start. Instead of coming along all conceited, he now sees his mistake and admits it.

> The Master pointed to the door. 'Go, get drunk on tea,'

Does that mean that Tokuzan accepted the monk's first answer?

'Go and get drunk on tea' means 'Go and meditate.'

That evening Sen took his tea to a quiet place and savoured it long and earnestly.

Normally we just accept everything we see, hear, feel or taste without being really aware of what is taking place. When we are born we don't know that we exist, we don't have a human consciousness yet. As the outside world begins to act on our sense organs, the contents of consciousness begin to develop. Through this contact of the external world with the interior world consciousness becomes adjusted. Through meditation and the associated awareness, one reaches an understanding of this process, instead of simply accepting what appears and becoming entangled in it. As a rule, we react to impressions with either pleasure or displeasure and form an opinion, but this judgement contains no insight, it is just our personal reaction to the occurrence. What actually happens is not understood at all. If for instance, I were to suddenly become deaf and had the wish to hear again, and with the help of a doctor this was actually made possible, then at the first sound or tone that I heard I would joyfully realise, 'I can hear again!' Then there would be no judgement of whether the sound pleased or displeased me. There would only be, 'Ah, I can hear.' Nothing more, nothing less.

The monk was asked to give himself into the meditation of drinking tea. In this case it is not a matter of the contact between the inside and outside through the ear or eye, but through the sense of taste. In Buddhism one identifies six senses and sense functions: touching, tasting, smelling, seeing, hearing and thinking. Just as one can comprehend something through the sense of touch, the eye or the ear, one can also establish contact through thinking and comprehend something. Contact is a fundamental principle of life. The most primitive life form, the amoeba, could not exist without contact with its environment. The sense of touch is the very first sense; everything else is built up on that.

So, the monk was told, 'Go and get drunk on tea.' – but he didn't go with that presumptuous, cocky attitude. He took his tea to a quiet place and savoured it long and earnestly.

He thought, 'It is not the taste that IS!'

The word 'IS' is written in capitals here. 'Is-ness' or suchness is an important matter in Zen. In the theory of knowledge 'is-ness' is the categorical imperative. To speak in the terms of Immanuel Kant, the father of Western epistemology, is-ness would be the noumenal from which the world of appearances is extracted.

He thought, 'It is not the taste that IS, nor the thing tasted,' – Salt is salty. There is the taste which is salty, and there is the substance which tastes like that, in this case the salt. Sugar tastes sweet. If our sense of taste were to change, then salt would suddenly no longer taste salty. Sugar no longer sweet. This young monk is now seriously pondering:

'It is not the taste that IS, nor the thing tasted, and yet what IS is all of these and all things else besides.'

One could object here that this all sounds very philosophical, but it isn't just philosophy. It is the realisation of how things really are. It is not imagining things, and it is not a theory. 'And yet, what IS is all of these and all things else besides.'

What is being described here is the following: When coming into contact with any object and becoming one with it, this object is then no longer an object. In this state – it is a state of meditation –

everything is truly one. Afterwards everything is differentiated again; the ear hears, the eye sees, the mind thinks; but one has experienced, sensed and realised that everything is essentially one. Here is a glass of water. The water is not me, and I am not the water. Yet I know that for the most part my body consists of water. I see the water and feel it, it has no smell and little taste, and sometimes I can hear it burbling. Now I drink it, and the water becomes one with my body, that is with me, because I and my body are identical. This water contributes to the survival of my body and therefore also my consciousness, including my I-consciousness. That is an entirely natural process. In meditation one becomes aware of this completely natural procedure, and in becoming one with the water physically as well as consciously, one reaches a totally different level of awareness. The unity between not-I (water) and I (body) is consciously experienced. That is why Sen Ts'en said, 'And yet what IS is all of these and all things else besides.' From physics and chemistry, we know that all substances, all things are differentiated energy. They are essentially all the same. There is an expression in Zen: 'When I sneeze here, a lion roars in Africa.' Of course, if I were in Africa and sneezed in the presence of a lion I would probably be gobbled up, but I'm here in Zürich and can sneeze without danger. Zen is a strange business…

Then suddenly it occurred to him that everything was other, and that this other was born and sustained and destroyed by something which was nothing.

That is a good description of how one uses the thinking mind in meditation. One must use thinking, because thinking is the springboard from which one jumps off into the pool of meditation. One jumps so to speak from thinking – but it must be real thinking – and dives into meditation. It shouldn't be a blind meditation, but a meditation in which there is an awareness. Ts'en thus realised that on the one hand something exists and on the other hand nothing exists – nothing. This nothing out of which everything arises, is not just emphasised in Zen, for in the *Tao-te-ching* Lao-tzu says, 'All things arise from being, but being arises from non-being.' When one meditates correctly, one first becomes aware of the world of appearances: this body with its hearing, feeling, thinking, etc. Then one moves on to withdrawing consciousness from the appearances and arrives at a state of Being. Changes are constantly occurring in the body, cells are destroyed and regenerate. One refers to this material change as metabolism. This process of change is our existence. Existence in turn rests in Being. This being should be experienced in meditation. After all it is there. Then one perceives that this being arises from non-being. All things return to this non-being, but they also emerge from it again, and become that which they already are. Out of an oak tree materialises an oak, out of a chicken a chicken materialises. It is understandable that many theories of reincarnation can be, and are, fabricated on this basis. These theories, however, are unimportant, and really have little meaning. If the objective is insight into the true nature of things, then it is unimportant whether one has lived a thousand times or just once. Every time the human form manifests itself, there is the opportunity through correct meditation to realise the true nature of things, to move from existence to being, that is to unity, and from being to non-being. 'Suddenly it occurred to him that everything was other, and that this other was born and sustained and destroyed by something which was nothing.'

Then rapt in this realisation he remained long in contemplation, and the following day he reported the experience to Tokuzan.

What comes next is typically Zen:

> The Master commended him…

That is suspicious, one has to be careful here when one is praised by a master.

> He said, 'You've done well. It took me ten years to arrive at such a realisation.'
> The monk was gratified.
> Then Tokuzan added, 'And another twenty more years before I could finally forget it.'

Yes, that's how it is. Humans dissect everything with their thinking. Dogs, birds and rabbits don't do this. Humans lose their unified consciousness by going into seeing, hearing, thinking, etc. And due to their desire to understand they analyse everything, whether it's in nature, medicine or any other field. One even does this with the psyche, and then believes to know what's going on with the soul. Perhaps one localises the seat of the soul in the brain, and the brain too can be analysed. Everything is dismantled into its component parts. But that gets nowhere near to explaining how the body, the soul, or the entire universe arrived at its symbiotic unity. Because first this unity has to be there – first the body is there, the psyche or the universe. How did this unity originate, what holds it together? Through meditation one aims to realise both aspects of existence, the world of appearances and the noumenal, reality as it functions. Both aspects are like the ends of a stick.

To experience the state of being is the easiest thing in meditation – after all one is always in it. One just has to stop rummaging about in thoughts, feelings and memories. Through our awareness all appearances come into existence. In deep sleep nothing exists – then everything is gone. As soon as I wake up everything is back again – past, future and present. We come out of non-existence into birth, step into the world of existence, become aware of it and die. This is happening continuously. For that there is no need to meditate.

Yet Tokuzan needed ten years to experience what the clever fellow experienced by drinking his tea. And then another twenty years to get rid of it. Someone who does not experiences the true Zen, I don't mean the Zen about which much is written or the Zen about which one has all kinds of ideas, but the correct, sober, dry Zen that is like the bleached bones of a skeleton, such a person should not rattle on about Zen. Zen is about a very specific realisation, and thus also about a very specific meditation. This tale of Tokuzan shows this very clearly: it proceeds from existence (Dasein) to Being (Sein) and from being to non-being. Yet no one wants to know about non-being; all want to get to being: 'In God's being I have eternal life.' In this eternity one naturally still is Mr. and Mrs. So-and-So. One wants to keep one's personality and identity for all time.

Whoever harbours such wishes should keep a distance from Zen. Zen is the poison the kills the individual. We as individuals are but appearances that have been assembled for a very brief time. I can't imagine anything worse than the notion that this body sitting, thinking and feeling here now would remain like this for all time. But there are also those who postulate that with the experiences of this life an individual can continue developing in a next life. They say, 'No, I'm not returning to this world, and I'm not going up to heaven. I'm going onto a different plane of consciousness. There I will cultivate myself further until I become a master. And as a master along with others who have become masters, I will guide the world.' That is a theosophical view. But all these notions are nothing but I-centred speculations. One should really desist from this identification with one's own person. In any case, that is the standpoint of Zen. What matters in Zen is to realise the Buddha-nature which is inherent in all of us, and in order to realise this true nature the identification with our own person has to be broken down. This means experiencing *kensho*, the insight into the original nature. This nature has absolutely nothing to do with the temporary, personal I. Every human being, every temporary individual has the opportunity to realise this Buddha-nature in this life. The way there is through correct, genuine meditation that leads away from I.

THE BEE

Sung was a scholar. As such he had studied Zen, but his intellect repelled against intuitive acceptance of irrational premises. Therefore he came to visit Tokuzan and asked, 'Is Zen compatible with rational presentation?'

'Zen is eating, Zen is sleeping, and what more rational would you wish?'

'This is what I mean,' said Sung. 'Your answer is no answer; your mouth opens and whole words come out.'

Tokuzan approved this remark. He said, 'True, it is that in the way of Zen reason and unreason walk as wondering ghosts, and words are the shades of shades. Therefore I would have you savour the moment direct, as a man who tastes his tea. Look!' He pointed to a bee about to alight.

Sung struck with a fan and the bee lay dead among scattered petals. 'What of the bee now, what of the moment, what of Zen?' He cried.

The Master looked on the little body with compassion. Then turning to the scholar, 'The cup is at the lips, but the contents spill all over the robe. You missed the flight of that bee, it flew by ages ago.'

The scholar was convinced. When he spoke his answer was no answer; his mouth opened and the words came out. 'The cherries in this garden are magnificent, they are blooms I would cultivate in my orchard.'

In its simplicity this story too is typical of Zen. There is nothing pretentious in it, nothing highbrow, no great philosophical constructions, no wonderful scientific theories, no religious ecstasy – it's simply about a bee, which is just about to alight on a flower, just as bees do.

In our Western world, which is more or less Christian-orientated – admittedly nowadays less than more – it is said that God created everything. In his totality this God stands over everything. He is transcendent. He is much more than that which he has created. God is so to speak the architect of the universe, and just as a human architect with his creative mind stands over his structure, so God stands over his creation. But at the same time God is also present in his creation, in each of his creatures, in all of nature – all-knowing and almighty. The bee belongs to nature. If God is immanent in his creation, then 'no bird falls from a branch without God knowing it.' God is in the bee. The bee, however, does not say, 'I am God.' It is a bee, looks like a bee and behaves like a bee.

Zen is not really that far removed from this Christian view in which God is understood as transcendent and immanent. True, Zen originated within the framework of Buddhism, but the essence and spirit (Geist) of Zen goes beyond this religious system. This essence or spirit can also be found in Islam or in Christianity or in the Indian traditions. Zen represents the innermost essence of all religions. When one traces the word 'religion' back to its origin, back to the Latin 'religare', then it means to re-link again with God or the truth or however you want to express it. Lucretius expressed it in the following way: 'The soul liberates itself by relinking with god.' The Indian term for this liberation is *mukti* or *moksha*. Of course, the idea of liberation also exists in Buddhism and in Islam.

'Sung was a scholar. As such he had studied Zen.' – Today one can read all kinds of things about Zen. But that is far from real Zen; those are just words, thoughts and ideas about Zen. Thoughts and words are not the thing itself. In this respect Zen is very simple: do it, don't talk about it, show it.

'But his intellect rebelled against intuitive acceptance of irrational premises.' – Many people, who look into Zen from an intellectual perspective, have the same difficulty. Their rational thinking hinders them from intuitively grasping the inconceivable. Bergson referred to the mental faculty that leads to the ability to grasp this as 'intellectual intuition'. This implies an ability to think which is not rational but intuitive. The great psychologist C.G. Jung identified four human personality types based on feeling, thinking sensation and intuition. In a person who is psychologically completely balanced, all these four functions would be evenly distributed. Generally, however, one or two of these functions predominate. Insight into one's own true nature requires intuition. Meister Eckhart said, 'The eye with which you see God is the same eye with which God sees you.' In order to understand this, one needs to use the intuitive faculty of the human being. With our two eyes we look out into the world and see things as they appear: large and small, beautiful and ugly, right and wrong, etc. But there is also seeing with the single eye. Many statues of the Buddha have a jewel on the forehead between the eyebrows as a symbol of the third eye. Seeing with the single eye is an intuitive perception of the innermost essence of existence. Lao-tzu said, that one can only perceive the essence of things with a non-desiring heart, whereas with a constantly desiring heart one only sees the outer shell of things.

'Sung rebelled against intuitive acceptance of irrational premises.' – According to C.G. Jung the collective unconscious is irrational in comparison with conscious thinking. Many dreams are irrational in this sense. Likewise in the dialogues between Zen masters or between Zen masters and their students much appears irrational. The same is true of koans. Through this irrationality one arrives at a higher rationality than that of our everyday thinking.

'Sung therefore came to visit Tokuzan and asked, "Is Zen comparable to rational presentation?" To which Tokuzan replied,

"Zen is eating, Zen is sleeping, and what more rational would you wish?"' – We mustn't forget that Sung was a scholar. He was in no way satisfied with this answer and said, '"This is what I mean. Your answer is no answer; your mouth opens and words come out." Tokuzan approved of this remark and said, "True it is that in the way of Zen reason and unreason walk as wandering ghosts, and words are the shades of shades."' – That is aptly expressed, rationality on the one hand and irrationality on the other hand and both walk about as wandering ghosts. Tokuzan continued, 'Therefore I would have you savour the moment direct, as a man who tastes his tea.' – Here is tea, drink it! It's nothing but tea. But who is it that drinks the tea? Clearly there is someone who sees, smells and tastes it, and sipping even hears it. They know it is tea, and can even use the word 'tea'. For one person the taste is to their liking, for another it is not. Who is it that perceives this? 'It's me, I'm drinking the tea.' What is it that says 'I'? Now this 'I' is in the act of drinking tea; then the tea is drunk and it's gone, but the 'I' is still there. Now the tea is part of myself, not just the water, but also the smell, the taste and the warmth. Obviously the tea and I have become united. But one usually doesn't reflect on this. Why should one ponder that – it's just nonsense? But in Zen one contemplates this. That is why Tokuzan says, 'You should savour the moment direct, as a man who tastes his tea with pleasure.' – Not like a dog or cat, but like a human. Being human is a spiritual matter, although at the same time it is also a material affair: tea, water, cup, mind (Geist) and matter combine, and if one's awareness is acute, *samjana* occurs, a becoming one with, or 'yoga' with the tea. In India from the earliest times, methods were developed to arrive at this state of becoming one.

Here is a string with wooden beads, Buddhist prayer beads, *japamala*. How can I become one with it? One could reflect on the symbolic meaning of this string of beads, that would be mentally becoming one. But one could also touch the beads individually or breathe in the fragrance of the wood. By integrating these prayer beads with meditation, so-called 'japa meditation', consciousness reaches a state, in which it penetrates the beads and dissolves the separation between 'I' and *mala*. One can also use the beads for reciting a mantra, as 'Namu Amida Butsu, namu Amida Butsu...' In this way one can also reach a state of meditation where there is no longer any difference between 'I' and the prayer beads. Both disappear in the oneness. In this unity both the 'I' and the string of beads have been transcended. Meditation is the simplest thing in the world. 'Reason and unreason walk as wandering ghosts, and words are shades of shades. Therefore I would have you savour the moment direct.' – At this moment: who are you? This moment: what is that? Tokuzan pointed at a bee and said, 'Look!' Just as the bee was about to alight on a flower, that idiot of a scholar struck it dead. He killed the bee and destroyed the flower with his intellectual arrogance. Thou shalt not kill says a commandment. It is a Jewish, a Christian and a Buddhist commandment.

'"What of the bee now, what of the moment, what of Zen?" cried Sung. The Master looked on the little body with compassion. Then turning to the scholar, "The cup is at the lips, but the contents spill all over the robe."' – Do you understand these words? The cup is a container for the tea. The human body is like a container for the spirit. The archetypical perception that God dwells within human beings is ancient and is not bound to any specific world religion. According to the Old Testament, God breathed his spirit into Adam and made him into a 'living soul', a *ruah*. Christ said, 'I am in you and you are in me.' In Buddhism the Buddha-nature is inherent in everyone, and the Indian religions regard the inner essence of man as divine.

The contents of the human body is of a spiritual nature. It should not be confused with the thoughts, sensations or feelings one has. What is being referred to here is pure spirit. If I am completely exhausted and drink a cup of tea, I am stimulated by the tea. That too is an example of the spiritual essence of the contents, because spirit also means life.

How can one drink tea if one is chatting at the same time? Instead of being completely aware of the tea, one is engaged in all kinds of other things. In Zen one is told, 'When drinking, then drink. When eating, then eat. When sleeping, then sleep. Whatever you do, be aware of it.' If you take away awareness, what have you got left? 'The cup is at the lips, but the contents spill all over the robe.' – And isn't it always like that as we run around in the history of the world? We have the cup at the lips, it is so close – and then the contents is spilled. Tokuzan added, 'You missed the flight of that bee; it flew by ages ago.' – The innermost essence of the manifestation of this form 'bee', the spirit of the bee, the living spirit of the bee was missed. In one brief moment – if we can grasp it – what we call past and future are united. The future which reaches far ahead, and the past which extends way back are present in this moment. This 'now', this moment is an eternal, everlasting 'now'. This can be demonstrated very simply and doesn't require any grand philosophical constructions. For example, how old is this sound? (Platov strikes the gong). It is now; it wasn't here before and soon it will fade away. How old is it? That is another one of those irrational Zen questions, isn't it? That sound already existed a very long time ago, and it will carry on ringing for a long, long time, if one realises that it is something spiritual. The audible sound and the inaudible sound are one. One realises this in meditation. But one shouldn't just meditate when doing zazen, one should use this spirit which is inherent in all of us in our ordinary daily life, in conscious at-one-ness with our working, sleeping, eating, drinking, hearing, seeing, thinking, feeling, etc. Everything takes place in this one spirit, and it is in everything that happens.

'You missed the flight of that bee; it flew by ages ago.' – How far back does this bee go? For how many centuries in our time reckoning will it carry on flying? What is it that is happening now when we don't divide it up into past, present and future? The past was once the present, the present will quickly turn into the past.

'The scholar was convinced.' – Now he had grasped something. 'When he spoke his answer was no answer; his mouth opened and the words came out. "The cherries in this garden are magnificent, they are blooms I would cultivate in my own orchard."' – Expressed symbolically consciousness is like a garden. In this garden there are many things: trees, flowers, bees, birds, shrubs. In a normal garden there are also what we designate as weeds. Cultivate your garden. Learn to distinguish between what appear to be weeds and real weeds, between seemingly valuable plants and really valuable plants. The garden of consciousness needs to be tended. Some things need to be planted in it and others need to be weeded out. One has to be able to discern what is worth keeping and what needs to be removed.

BIRTH OF A DRAGON

This next story from the Tales of Tokuzan is quite interesting, but at the same time it is also rather difficult to understand. It shows the Taoist character of Zen. In China the dragon is a very important symbol. There it has a positive meaning, in contrast to the West where the dragon is seen mostly in a negative light. The same applies to the serpent which is interpreted positively in Eastern esoterism, but negatively in the Judaic-Christian religion.

T'zun, the priest of Tao, called on Tokuzan. He said, 'I have previously profited by your teaching. Will you now kindly tell me, without equivocation, what it is that is?'

Tokuzan replied, 'I cannot say it for another, but here is my stanza:

Face downwards, I lie in the mud,
Spread-eagled, for endless ages.
With fertilisation such as this,
Spring flowers grow in profusion.'

'May I know the meaning of the stanza?' said T'zun?

Tokuzan replied, 'Only when you understand your own, can you know the meaning of mine. However, I will endeavour to enlighten you. One thought follows another. Tell me, what at this moment comes into your mind?'

'One thought follows another,' said T'zun, plodding in the footsteps of the Master.

'In the manner of …?'

'Fruit ripens and falls,' continued T'zun, perceiving now his own particular path.

'Then what would you say…?'

'Lying on my back, I watch fruit ripen.' This time the spirit soars.

'Is that all?'

'Lying on my back, I watch fruit ripen. Do I but yawn, it drops right into my mouth.'

No priest is there now, nor path indeed, but a dragon flying high.

Tokuzan called his attendant. 'Bring fruit and cakes and tea,' he said, 'our guest has travelled far.'

What sort of verse would you make out of this story, if I were to stop now without giving a commentary? The point is to compose a verse as an expression of insight. In Sanskrit such a verse is called a *gatha*. What would someone who just read or heard these lines understand? Perhaps they would try and understand it on the basis of a certain feeling that was aroused by it or try and grasp it intellectually.

Tokuzan met his guest on T'zun's own ground, almost accompanied him hand in hand. This kind or encounter is very important. It is as if Tokuzan were saying, 'I don't wish to impose anything of mine on you. You have to come to an insight from within yourself. You shouldn't just accept what someone else is trying to convince you of without it being your own understanding.' So Tokuzan put himself in the other's shoes and tried to see things from a Taoist priest's point of view.

T'zun asked Tokuzan, 'I have previously profited by your teaching. Will you now kindly tell me, without equivocation, what it is that is?' – There is a very simple way to answer such questions. What is this? (Platov points to a wooden staff on the table.) It is a piece of wood. It once was a tree. There are probably many pieces of wood from this tree. From a scientific perspective one could say that it is a specific molecular structure, or taken a step further it can be seen as a manifestation of energy. Someone else might say, 'It is an object that according to my consciousness I see in this way. If I had different eyes or a flaw in my perception, the object would be different. Hence, I don't know what it is.' A Zen master would not answer like that. Perhaps he might just say the following: (Platov whacks the table with the wooden staff.) Though the question has been answered, who would be able to understand this answer? The answer has become a koan. But T'zun wanted an answer without any equivocation. How did Tokuzan respond to this wish, to explain to T'zun without equivocation what it is that is? Tokuzan replied, 'I cannot say it for another, but here is my stanza:

> Face downwards, I lie in the mud,
> Spread-eagled, for endless ages.
> With fertilisation such as this,
> Spring flowers grow in profusion.'

You have to understand that that according to Taosim man exists between heaven and earth. That is very realistic. From the earth he receives his nourishment and on its surface he moves and rests. Above him is heaven with its life-giving light. Through his upright gait man is oriented upwards and strives towards the heavenly. Symbolically the earth is associated with the material and heaven with the spiritual. And correspondingly Taoist meditation is earth-bound – it is not a meditation whereby one loses oneself on the seventh pink cloud in the sky, but a meditation that begins with earth-consciousness and builds on that. In Tantra too this earth-consciousness is emphasised.

When T'zun asked about the meaning of the verse, Tokuzan said, 'Only when you understand your own, can you know the meaning of mine.' – Realisation has to be in oneself. When two people, in this case T'zun and Tokuzan, realise the same thing, they are one. Then there is no longer a separation. That is the hidden aim of the *mondo*, the characteristic question and answer dialogues of Zen, out of which the koan developed. Koans are not riddles as they are often referred to in the abundant literature now available on Zen. The one who asks and the one who answers become one in the same consciousness. Figuratively this is expressed as 'rubbing eyebrows'. If you imagine two heads nodding close to one another, bushy eyebrows touching, then you've got the image. This mutual understanding embraces all levels of encounter: a physical, mental and spiritual coming together.

Under the pretext of offering an explanation, Tokuzan now introduces a *mondo*. He says, 'One thought follows another. Tell me, what thought at this moment comes into your mind?' – There is a very similar koan which asks: 'At this very moment, without thinking yes or no, what are you thinking?' One thought follows another, we all know that. Even in meditation the chain of thoughts passes in front of us without interruption. We are, as it were, caught in it. Yet one has to interrupt this chain. Break through it, somewhere, at any point! Only that way can we escape its pull. To try and make an effort not to think is futile. But one does have the choice of letting oneself be caught by the thoughts or not. Instead of being caught by them, just give them free rein. One thought follows another, but what does it have to do with me?

'In what manner does one thought follow another?' – Tokuzan's question motivates T'zun to search for his own way. A koan always poses a direct question: You, who are sitting here now, what do *you* say, give me your own answer!

There is a koan that asks: 'How is it that a monk can walk by putting one foot in front of the other?' When walking, one leg follows the other. How? In what manner? To this question Gustav Meyrink told the following story: Once upon a time there was a centipede and a frog. The frog always watched the centipede moving elegantly in the sunshine, whereas he himself was so awkward. He grew so envious of the centipede that he could hardly bear it any longer. He dived deep down into the pond to speak to an old frog and said, 'This centipede moves so elegantly with so much agility, that I'm getting ill with envy. What can I do about it?' So the old frog told him what he should do. The next day as the frog was sitting on his lily pad the centipede passed by again. The frog addressed him saying, 'Oh, you glisten so beautifully in the sunlight and meander along so gracefully, whereas I can only hop along. Please tell me how you do that, which foot do you move first when you walk?' The centipede sat down and considered which foot he would move first to get going, and because he remained motionless for so long while he was contemplating this, he was burnt by the rays of the sun. – How can a monk walk, putting one foot in front of the other?

Once when I'd given my teacher Sokei-an an answer to a koan, he asked me how I had arrived at this answer. 'Through thought association,' I said. He shouted at me, 'Stop this nonsense and get out of here, you fool!'

'"In what manner does one thought follow another?" asked Tokuzan. "Fruit that ripens and falls," continued T'zun, perceiving now his own particular path.' – Tokuzan had said, 'Face downwards, I lie in the mud, spread-eagled for endless ages. With fertilisation such as this, spring flowers grow in profusion.' That was Tokuzan's path. Now T'zun saw his own path. It was now no longer just Tokuzan's verse, but also T'zun's verse, the same understanding, the same insight, the same knowledge.

'"Then what would you say…?" prompted Tokuzan. And now T'zun shows Tokuzan his insight. "Lying on my back, I watch fruit ripen. Do I but yawn, it drops right into my mouth." No priest is there now, nor path indeed, but a dragon flying high.' – First there was the fertilisation, 'Face downwards, I lie in the mud, spread-eagled for endless ages...' Then there was the growth of the fruit and watching it ripen.

When one practises zazen one should be aware of the entire depth and weight of the earth under one's meditation cushion and of the lightness of the heavens on one's shoulders. Lao-tzu said, 'Heaviness is the root of lightness...' The treetop that reaches up to heaven and sways gently back and forth is held by the root which is anchored into the earth. That is why in Zen meditation the focus is placed on the lower abdomen. You can experiment and observe that an upright standing person is, as a rule, easy to pick up. Yet as soon as that person concentrates on their lower abdomen, on the *hara*, it is almost impossible to lift them. 'Heaviness is the root of lightness...' and further on, 'Tranquillity is the master of movement.' There is meditation in tranquillity and meditation in movement. Why can a monk put one foot in front of the other? A monk, that is a human being, who doesn't just wander through the world unconsciously, should know how it is that they can put one foot before the other.

'Lying on the stomach...' – facing the earth – 'Lying on the back...' – facing heaven. There is the power of the earth, the root strength, which nourishes everything, and there is the heavenly power, which draws up everything that sprouts out of the earth. The root strives downwards into the darkness, the blossom strives upwards towards the light. Every flower has a root, a stem and a blossom. This applies to humans too, they have a root, a stem and a blossom. The lotus flower has its root in the dark mud, but its blossom is pure white. The mire is an image of the *dharmakaya*, that body of the Buddha out of which everything arises. A fruitful Zen training leads to the realisation of the *dharmakaya*.

To find the earth consciousness within oneself one has to turn inwards and remove the projections which turn to the outside. Then,

'Lying on my back, I watch the fruit ripen. Do I but yawn, it drops right into my mouth.' In the book, *The Secret of the Golden Flower,* this Taoist meditation is described very clearly.

Pure observation as it is practised in Vipassana, for example, is a very good meditation practise. By that practice one can distance oneself from the inner processes and ultimately discover the observer. In the *Bhagavad-Gita* the observer is described as a passenger sitting in a coach. He has nothing to do with the coach, nor with the horse that pulls the coach and also not with the coachman who takes care of the horse and the coach. The passenger just sits there and observes.

In Taoism there is the principle of *wei wu-wei*, the doing in not-doing. It refers to what occurs of itself and is not controlled by 'I'. Naturally this relates to almost all expressions of existence. 'Do I but yawn, it drops right into my mouth.' One is completely relaxed when yawning.

'No priest is there now, nor path indeed....' Everyone is somehow searching for a path, but should realise that they are themselves the path. There is no 'I and the path'. When I and the path are one, then there is neither an I nor a path; that is the fifth position of meditation.

'No priest is there now, nor path indeed, but a dragon flying high.' The most popular image of the dragon in China is the one where the dragon rises out of the deep mountain lake and spewing fire, soars high into the heavens. In Buddhism it is said that one has to be reborn out of water and fire. Jesus said to Nicodemus, 'You must be reborn out of water and spirit.' In the Indian tradition *agni*, fire, is a symbol for spirit. And the dragon is a symbol for this second birth.

In esotericism it is said that one must liberate oneself from earth consciousness. But that is of course not correct. There can be no water without a container. The mountain is a container for water. It would be wrong to say that the ascent of the dragon out of the water represents the liberation from earth consciousness. According to the Taoist teachings one has to penetrate the earth consciousness and then rise up from there. Human beings exist between heaven and earth. They are not bipartite, they are a unity like heaven and earth. The one emerges from the other. Heraclitus spoke of *enantiodromia*, the merging and flowing into one another of opposites. The Chinese *t'ai chi* symbol, the circle with the black and white parts, shows the merging of opposites.

'Tokuzan called his attendant. "Bring fruit and cakes and tea," he said. "Our guest has travelled far."'– In his encounter with Tokuzan T'zun undertook a great journey. If you leave it to nature to attain an insight, it can take half an eternity. But if one meditates properly and hopefully with correct guidance, then it shouldn't take half an eternity, but at most half a lifetime. That should suffice if one really buckles down to it.

THE DREAM

The following story of Tokuzan is perhaps a little difficult to understand. It is called The Dream.

> A monk dreamed he was on an island surrounded by rising waters. Suddenly the vision cleared, and he found himself brush in hand facing paper and ink. Reflecting that he must have fallen asleep in the act of writing, he began to muse on the nature of reality and the distinction between dreaming and waking, seeking to fathom the philosophical implications of the state of being.
>
> While thus engaged he again awoke, and found that the first dream had merged into a second.
>
> Marvelling at the mystery of mind, he went to Tokuzan and asked him to explain.
>
> The Master called for tea, and poured out two cups. Then he said, 'Two states or conditions are peculiar to mind-only. First there is the arising of discrimination between sleeping and waking, then there is the cessation of discrimination. Meantime the tea cools, waiting to be drunk. Now, what would you say?'
>
> The monk's brow wrinkled as he considered the question.
>
> Tokuzan remarked, 'The tiger is lashing his tail before he begins his leap.'
>
> The monk's brow cleared as he took his cup of tea.
>
> Tokuzan smiled benignly. 'The tiger has filled his belly before he begins to feed.'

'A monk dreamed he was on an island surrounded by rising waters.' – From the perspective of depth psychology, one could say that this was an archetypical dream. In a sense, every human being in his individuality, in his I-ness is an island surrounded by water. Archetypically water can be seen as consciousness, and rising water would, according to this, be an expanding consciousness. In the Christian tradition, for example, there is the image of the baptism of Jesus, in which Jesus does not sink into the water, but the water rises up to him. That is a primordial image (Urbild) with a very specific meaning: one delves down into the deeper consciousness whereby consciousness itself rises up. One can actually experience this, it is a delving down that is a rising up. This is what the monk experienced in his dream.

'Suddenly the vision cleared, and he found himself brush in hand facing paper and ink. Reflecting that he must have fallen asleep in the act of writing, he began to muse on the nature of reality and the distinction between dreaming and waking, seeking to fathom the philosophical implications of the state of being.' – It is completely natural for us to dream. But one can also ask oneself what the difference is between dreaming and being awake. In any case, this monk asked himself that question. He reflected. There is a state of being – one is there – and within it there is a waking state and a dream state. Usually, we see the awake state as real and the dream state as unreal and generally it is very easy to tell the two apart. But sometimes the two merge, the dream passes over into the waking state or the waking state passes into the dream. That really happens, everyone can experience that. So the monk reflected, and 'while thus engaged he again awoke, and found that the first dream had merged into a second.' Both the vision of the island with the rising water and the reflection on the essence of reality revealed themselves to be a dream. 'Marvelling at the mystery of mind, he went to Tokuzan and asked him to explain. The Master called for tea, and poured out two cups. Then he said, "Two states or conditions are peculiar to mind-only."' –

I have to explain this term 'mind-only'.

There are two major schools within the Indian Mahayana tradition, the Yogacara- and the Madhyamika School. The Yogacara School is a quasi-esoteric philosophical school founded by Asanga and Vasubandhu. They taught that all that exists is 'mind-only', meaning that all forms of existence are only phenomena in the mind and that everything that we see, hear, our entire thinking and our sensations are all just representations. There is nothing apart from the pictures of the mind. The mind is the only thing that exists. Outside of mind there is nothing. What Tokuzan explains here, comes out of the Yogacara teaching: 'Two states or conditions are peculiar to mind-only. First there is the arising of discrimination between sleeping and waking…' – When one sleeps without dreaming, the I-consciousness is gone. When one dreams, it is one with the dream, yet sometimes one knows one is dreaming. When awake the I-consciousness is there – I am awake – but it usually gets lost amid what is happening.

'…secondly there is the cessation of discrimination.' – What does that mean? If I sleep without dreaming, there is no difference between sleeping and waking. Afterwards when I wake up, I say: now I'm awake again. But it is a mistake to consider one real and the other not. Being awake and dreaming belong to the same reality of Being. Seen from the perspective of 'mind-only' there is no difference between a waking dream and a sleeping dream, both are dreams. They are activities of the same mind. That is the 'cessation of discrimination'. A waking dream and a sleeping dream are two sides of a coin, either one keeps the two sides separate, or one doesn't differentiate and sees the sameness of both states.

The other major school, the Madhyamika School, was founded by Nagarjuna. It is not so esoterically orientated – it is the school of the Middle Way. At its foundation is Nagarjuna's great equation: samsara is nirvana, that is, samsara and nirvana are identical. Zen belongs to this school. Zen does agree with the Yogacara that our world is a world of phenomena, because we only see it as we see it since our sense organs are conditioned accordingly. But Zen doesn't radically maintain that all phenomena are only mind, but regards our world of phenomena, samsara, as an aspect of reality, nirvana.

Now Tokuzan takes the next step by saying, 'Meantime the tea cools, waiting to be drunk. Now, what would you say?' – With that he takes a Zen position and changes over from the Yogacara thinking to the Madhyamika view. Here we are talking about the waking- and the dream-state, all the while the tea is waiting to be drunk. So do I say, 'The tea is cooling down, I want to drink it before it gets cold.' Or does the tea say, 'Drink me before I get cold.'? How is that? What is the difference between the tea out there in the cup and the tea inside me? Is it a unity or a duality? When one sees that inside and outside are the same, then one understands Nagarjuna's equation.

Both the Yogacara and the Madhyamika schools have the same goal, namely the realisation of nirvana. In the Yogacara School this raises the question of whether mind which exists alone, 'mind-only', is nirvana or not, for in this school the equation samsara equals nirvana does not pertain. How can one find nirvana in 'mind-only'? With this question the two schools can engage in philosophical debate. But from a Zen perspective it is not a problem at all, because in Zen one doesn't approach the question philosophically. The koan reads as folllows: Find nirvana in the world of phenomena. That is why Tokuzan asks, 'Now, what would you say?'

'The monk's brow wrinkled as he considered the question.' – Meanwhile Tokuzan observed him and remarked, 'The tiger is lashing his tail before he begins his leap.' – The tiger is an oft used symbol in Zen. The great severe Master Nanshinken was referred to as 'tiger', and in confronting such a master one says that the monks pull the tiger by his whiskers. That is an extremely difficult thing to do and only a very advanced student can pull the whiskers of the tiger. The tail of a tiger is also important, for observing the tail one knows when the tiger is about to pounce. And to grasp the tiger by the tail can be very dangerous. All of these images come from the confrontation between master and pupil. Most monks are not tigers yet, at most they have a cow's tail. It takes quite a while before a cow is transformed into a tiger, that is, before cow-meditation becomes the meditation of tiger. Cow-meditation is meditation without realisation and is an allusion to the seemingly vacant stare of the cow's eyes.

'The monk's brow cleared as he took his cup of tea.' – Now he understood how the nature of reality functions. Gustav Meyrink used to tell the story of a little lion cub who was raised by an ewe and wandered about with a flock of sheep. One day he encountered a lion. The lion looked at him and the cub said, 'Baa-aa-aa.' The lion, rather puzzled, just stared at him, whereupon the lion cub again said, 'Baa-aa-aa.' Then the old lion gave a loud lion's roar – and for the first time the lion cub heard the sound of its own nature. This is a typical Meyrink story. So the lion began to recognise its own nature, just like the Zen student does through the koan: 'What was your true nature before mother and father were born?'

In the Yogacara one accepts everything one sees, hears and feels, everything within oneself as representation of mind. By contrast the Madhyamika School, especially as expressed in Zen, is more rigorous. There the emphasis is placed on seeing through the world of phenomena and understanding what it is based on; and all the while the master stands next to one ready to strike with his stick.

My teacher, Sokei-an, once found a very beautiful stone, flat on the bottom and rounded on top. He wrote 'This is nirvana' on the stone and used it as a paperweight. – What is reality? What is waking, sleeping, dreaming….? To see the unity of nirvana and samsara, that is what concerns Zen.

'Tokuzan smiled benignly. "The tiger has filled his belly before he begins to feed."' – He had filled his meditation-belly, his *hara*. One gobbles up all kinds of things, with the mouth, as well as with the eyes, the ears and the mind. But the tiger digests very well, he has a strong stomach. Someone who has a good hara can digest everything they consume. But for those with a weak hara, much remains difficult to digest. Cows are ruminant, and those who meditate like cows, have to chew things over again and again. Hopefully one day they will grow weary of this continuous ruminating, cut it off and become a tiger instead.

Since there is war everywhere nowadays (1985), it is quite
appropriate to hear what Tokuzan has to say about it.

'You monks know the maxim: "No enemy under Heaven".
What do you think it means? Not one of you but now
begins to puzzle his brains, sunk up to his shaven hairs in
the embarrassment of intellection. It means no enemy under
Heaven.

'You look at me, suspecting tricks, a play on words and
the like. Why should I try to deceive those who have not yet
given a sign? This enemy – where is he, what is he? Robber
Chang and his hordes? Emperor Chou and his hosts? Are
these your enemies? Our lands are laid waste, our granaries
are burned, our monasteries despoiled. Did an enemy do this?
Listen to my stanza:

> Under stress of storm of fresh eager impetus of new life,
> Trees lose their leaves;
> Yet when men lose their reason
> Others upbraid them! I will tell you what warfare
> is; dried leaves blown across the courtyard; that and
> nothing more.

'What then is to be done? We sweep the leaves, we
pause from our labours, as and when occasion arises. And
meanwhile what occupies our thoughts? The koan. Yet have
I not heard you polluting the air in the recreation hall with
poisonous miasmas that you call plans for the reconstructions
of a brave new world when Robber Chang and Emperor

Chou confine their activities to spasmodic movements on the end of a long string? Would you bring your visions to earth and give them form and substance? Babes that you are! Do you not know that the forms of your dreams would remain substantial as sandcastles on the beach, the sport of each tide of circumstances in the rhythm of its coming and going? Tides flow, leaves fall, in the appointed and inevitable hour. Likewise, your enemies, or those whom you so designate, fall upon you, and with similar significance. When they kill you, the gust of wind has blown the leaf a little farther, that is all.

'Enemies? I say you have no enemies, you have but teachers, as mountains and mists, pines and the waning moon teach you, all in season. When sweat pours, you wipe your face; when thirst prompts, you drink your fill; when hostilities cease, you hew fresh rafters and replace broken tiles. So inevitable, so ordinary, so far from the minds of monks who, being babes, should know better. The afternoon is oppressive. My discourse is ended.'

So-So stepped forward and said, 'The master's mouth is full of pus. He treads the razor-edge with the agility of a fallen tree. He offends us by comparing us to babes when we still kick in the womb. He says, "No enemy under Heaven." I point to Robber Chang and Emperor Chou. He asks, "Why make plans?" I say we make plans.'

So-So then stepped back into his place. Later, Tokuzan called So-So to his room. 'What have we? What do we make?' he asked. So-So gave no answer. 'Oh, Robber Chang,' murmured the Master, 'do you too despoil me?'

This is a long story. The original text is even longer as the author added more comments, which I haven't read out, but will cite in my own commentary. In the *Bhagavad Gita* the god Krishna speaks to Arjuna, that is, to the soul and says, 'You have to fight your enemies that surround you.' The *Bhagavad Gita* is perhaps the most important section of the well-known great epic *Mahabharata*. Everyone who is interested in religious philosophy whether a Buddhist, Hindu, Sufi or Christian should read and study this text. The enemies that surround Arjuna are the enemies in himself. He has to engage in mortal combat with them. Yet Arjuna refuses to accept this, saying, 'But these enemies are my relatives, my friends and associates.' But Krishna insists that they are enemies and that Arjuna must fight them. He has to wage war against them. If one wanted to express this in terms of our Western psychology, one would say that all the enemies outside ourselves are the projections of our inner enemies. If one can't get along with oneself, then one has difficulty relating to others and blames them for it. If the other person also can't get along with themselves, they also project the cause of their difficulties on others, and then you have hostility on both sides. Actually, such personal matters are totally meaningless and unimportant, yet they lead to conflict and war. One has to recognise the true cause within oneself and then fight these inner enemies. But instead, everything is rationalised politically and economically and real conflicts are kindled. What is really behind these wars is never really revealed. Because every individual belongs to the collective, everyone is jointly responsible for what happens in the collective. From the Buddhist viewpoint we are all karmically responsible for what happens in the world. Buddhist ethics are very far-reaching. It is not just a matter of living according to the precepts. What each individual thinks and does has repercussions on everyone and everything. Buddhist ethics are so encompassing that my teacher, Sokei-an, once said that it is very difficult to be a true Buddhist, just as it is difficult to be a real Christian. Through our actions and thoughts, we are responsible for the actions and thoughts of everyone else. How many people are we? Countless come and go, birth and death alternate with one another continuously. However, in the truest sense of the word, there is only one human being; the many individuals are all one. Only by first overcoming oneself, can one help others to overcome themselves.

As you know, there are two major schools in Buddhism: the Hinayana, known as the 'Small Vehicle' and the Mahayana, the so-called 'Great Vehicle'. In Hinayana or Theravada Buddhism one strives for the goal of arhat; in the Mahayana one follows the bodhisattva ideal. The arhat who has attained the highest insight remains in an enlightened state with the gaze averted from the world, while the bodhisattva returns to the world to assist sentient beings to also attain enlightenment. The Buddha attained great enlightenment – *anuttara samyak sambodhi* – and then until the end of his life showed others the way he had found. Seen in this way, he was a bodhisattva.

I will now start with the story of Tokuzan. 'You monks know the maxim: "No enemy under Heaven". What do you think it means? Not one of you but now begins to puzzle his brains, sunk up to his shaven hairs in the embarrassment of intellection. It means no enemy under Heaven.' – In other words, don't concern yourselves with it. It is quite simple, there is no enemy.

'You look at me, suspecting tricks, a play on words and the like. Why should I try to deceive those who have not yet given a sign?' – Those who have not given any sign of understanding. When the Buddha gave his famous Flower Sermon, in which he said not one word and only held up a flower, none of those present understood. Only Mahakasyapa understood and showed it with a certain smile.

'This enemy – where is he, what is he?' – Are Robber Chang and Emperor Chou, whose hordes lay waste to the land as they march through the region plundering and burning, really your enemies? Then Tokuzan composed a verse in which he showed what he really felt about war:

> 'Under stress of storm of fresh eager impetus of new life,
> Trees lose their leaves;
> Yet when men lose their reason
> Others upbraid them!'

What does it mean to 'lose one's reason'? Does it mean to become mentally ill or to go daft? No. Earlier, Tokuzan said that the monks had sunk into the embarrassment of intellection. When one really practises meditation, one can't help but lose this reason. The realisation of real truth goes beyond reasonable thinking. With this kind of meditation, one becomes like a withered tree, without thoughts or wishes. And then? Then a new life awakens in this tree. Blossoms and leaves grow again. One has to experience that in order to understand it.

'When men lose their reason, others upbraid them.' – We become attached to our own thoughts, our own words and expect others to acknowledge these thoughts and words. If one doesn't take part, one gets upbraided.

'I will tell you what warfare is; dried leaves blown across the courtyard; that and nothing more.' – There are some who are of the opinion that monks who just meditate without participating or engaging in what is happening in the world are wasters and basically worthless, because they are only interested in their own enlightenment and live at the expense of others. They regard it as selfishness to just strive for the realisation of the truth. Nowadays there is an opposite view proposing that through group meditation the consciousness of the surroundings can be changed. If I were asked if that was true, I would say, 'no'. One shouldn't try and sell the idea of meditation by saying, 'If you all get together and meditate, it won't just benefit yourselves but the environment too.' Hiding behind this sales tactic is just wishful thinking. Thereby one can also rationalise away the criticism and justify one's non-engagement in the world, by maintaining that through meditation one can help others reach a higher state of consciousness. But that is not what happens. No one helps others simply by meditating. If we had a large gong here and would strike it early in the morning for our meditation practice, the neighbours would become suspicious and wonder what was going on here. The ringing of church bells is acceptable, but such an exotic thing as the sound of an oriental gong, that is just not done....

When meditating together, each individual should only be concerned with their own zazen. Everyone has their own koan, and is their own koan. One shouldn't be worried about the person sitting next to or across from one: 'Am I meditating better than them? Are they getting on with their koan better than I am with mine?' All that kind of I-orientation has to be given up. Why then sit together at all and not just sit on one's own? One does have to be able to sit on one's own as well, but communal zazen has its own meaning. But the way it functions is not to be found on the surface. Each person sits alone and has their own problems to work through, just like trees in a garden. They all stand there separately, but their roots are embedded in the same ground. We meditate together in order to arrive at the same ground! On the surface we all appear to be different, just like the trees, but in the ground we are one. It is not the consciousness of the environment that changes, but our own consciousness should change.

How does an arhat influence others? Actually, he isn't even interested in influencing others. He goes his own way upwards. Having vowed to bring all beings to enlightenment, how does a bodhisattva influence others? He doesn't impose himself on people and say, 'My view is the right one, I will correct your false views.' The influence is not on the surface, it doesn't consist of words. It lies completely under the surface.

One has to differentiate between what takes place on the surface and in the environment and what happens underneath the surface. One can't go around saying, 'I'm a Buddhist or Zen practitioner and I have to show people which is the right way.' In that case, you're a fine one to talk! One shouldn't just look at what someone else is doing and think, 'With me it's different.' It's not different at all. We are all exactly the same. Jesus said, 'Why do you look at the speck of sawdust in your brother's eye and pay no attention to the plank in your own eye?'

Gathered in this room, we are also in a kind of courtyard, a Zen courtyard.

'Dried leaves are blown across a courtyard,' that is war, nothing more. In each one of you a war is taking place in thoughts, feelings, etc. Everyone can observe this in themselves. They are dried leaves. Yet we transfer this war, which we conduct in ourselves, onto others and thus it becomes a collective happening. We know well enough how we rationalise and justify these wars.

'What then is to be done? We sweep the leaves, we pause from our labours, as and when occasion arises. And meanwhile what occupies our thoughts? The koan. Yet have I not heard you polluting the air in the recreation hall with poisonous miasmas that you call plans for the reconstructions of a brave new world....' – How well we can delude ourselves – building a brave new world! '...when Robber Chang and Emperor Chou confine their activities to spasmodic movements on the end of a long string? Would you bring your visions to earth and give them form and substance? Babes that you are! Do you not know that the forms of your dreams would remain substantial as sandcastles on the beach, the sport of each tide of circumstances in the rhythm of its coming and going? Tides flow, leaves fall, in the appointed and inevitable hour...' – Buddha founded his teaching on this impermanence. Everything arises and passes away, and is, in this coming to be and ceasing to be, actually of no consequence. If, when practising meditation, one resists the urge to indulge in illusions, then it is possible to see that coming and going, right and wrong, good and bad, beautiful and ugly, are all quite irrelevant as such, and that it really only comes down to one thing, namely, that within this coming and going one grasps that which neither comes to be nor ceases to be. But people who are caught up in their own and in collective values, judge this meditation as selfish. According to their opinion one has to engage in world events; in their ignorance they don't realise that they keep getting stuck in the same rut again and again. Tokuzan describes the activities of Robber Chang and Emperor Chou as 'spasmodic movements on the end of a long string.' Don't you know that a Robber Chang and an Emperor Chou dwell in you and do nothing more than create the undulations of a string? That is a good image of the state we find ourselves in.

'Do you not know that the forms of your dreams would remain substantial as sandcastles on the beach...' – We know what happens to sandcastles on the beach, the waves come and wash them away. 'Tides flow, leaves fall, in the appointed and inevitable hour. Likewise, your enemies, or those whom you so designate, fall upon you, and with similar significance. When they kill you, the gust of wind has blown the leaf a little farther, that is all.' – It is only possible to understand this statement from the perspective of true meditation, that is, from the position of samadhi. When one reaches samadhi through correct meditation, one sees that it is just like it is described here.

Tokuzan continues: 'Enemies? I say you have no enemies.' – On the one hand there are enemies to fight, and then on the other hand there are no enemies. 'You have but teachers, as mountains and mists, pines and the waning moon teach you, all in season. When sweat pours, you wipe your face; when thirst prompts, you drink your fill; when hostilities cease, you hew fresh rafters and replace broken tiles.'

– We can also observe this nowadays wherever there are wars. 'So inevitable, so ordinary, so far from the minds of monks who, being babes, should know better. The afternoon is oppressive. My discourse is ended.' – If I now take up Tokuzan's position and appear as the devil's advocate, I will say to you, 'All of your sitting is completely worthless. All this grappling with koans is futile. Why not simply live as you came into the world?' One is born, soils one's nappies and sucks at one's mother's breast. One grows into adulthood, but still remains an infant. One goes on sucking at all kinds of things and the mind soils nappies just like the newborn infant. The mind should not be a sieve through which everything flows out. You listen to Zen lectures and read the sutras, and the mind greedily soaks it all up, but before long it lets it all go again. Zen masters are sometimes really mean, they hurl insults at people.

This reminds me of a well-known American writer who addresses numerous social and scientific themes. According to his thinking, he is a communist and socially engaged, but he has also given considerable time and thought to Zen. He is a very intelligent person who is also very concerned about the 'weal and woe' of others. His conclusion about Zen was: 'Zen is a stench in the world.' From an idealistic point of view, what Tokuzan says here could also be referred to as stinking Zen. It doesn't help anyone. Wars are waged, people are killed and mutilated, famines are brought about and then someone like Tokuzan comes along and says it's all just 'spasmodic movements on the end of a long string' or 'dried leaves blown across the courtyard.' Yes, seen from this standpoint, that writer is completely in the right when he says that Zen stinks.

The Christian religion helps people, it goes out and tries to lighten the suffering of human beings, that has to be acknowledged. Buddhism doesn't do that. It holds the view that people bring about their own suffering and therefore have to help themselves. It is the concern of politics to care for the well-being of its citizens, not the concern of religion. Pure religion doesn't have anything to do with the goings-on among people. When they fight with one another or suffer the consequences of natural catastrophes, they have to help one another to the best of their abilities – this happens quite naturally and has no need for religion. This brings us to the question of humanism and religion. Religion as religion is simply religion, nothing more. Is there something like a humanistic religion? Christianity is described as a humanistic religion, but when looking deeper into it, it isn't humanistic. For example, Jesus said, 'Let the dead bury the dead.' The purely religious element in all religions is not humanistic, it goes beyond the humane. Let me repeat: after wars and catastrophes people have to help one another – they have to hew fresh rafters and replace broken tiles. Yet within these everyday events, within one's own self and in relation to others, each individual has to strive to realise the truth. That holds true for all religions. In Catholicism there are monks, in Buddhism and also in Indian ashrams. In religion the main concern is to realise the truth, and everything else that happens, including death, is nothing but dried leaves blown across the courtyard. So I would like to repeat that if one really practises Zen meditation, one becomes like a withered tree that loses its leaves and then out of an inner strength renews itself. That is why this meditation is referred to as dying, a dying off. But this dying doesn't pertain just to Zen, it is also known in the Christian religion. St. Paul said, 'I die daily.' What did he mean by that? To understand this, we could sit down and like St. Paul say, 'I die daily. Here I sit, breathe, live, think, feel, and know what is going on around me, but I'm dying.' That would be a useful meditation theme. Perhaps another life will emerge from this dying. But not as Tokuzan says it so well here: 'Yet have I not heard you polluting the air in the recreation hall with poisonous miasmas that you call plans for the reconstructions of a brave new world?'

We now come to the second part of the story where Tokuzan and So-So mirror one another.

'So-So stepped forward and said, "The master's mouth is full of pus."' – Tokuzan in his entirety is like a tumour. In the text there now follows a commentary as an aside by the storyteller, Gabb, who says: 'Why not? Pus is as pleasing to the eye as cream. Not until the truth is known does the stomach turn; so with many words. Superficially they may be very sound, but when we know the truth then giving it a name is objectionable, and verbosity is vomit.' – When we look closely at everything that is going on inside our bodies, we sometimes can feel physically sick. In old Japan, that is, in Japan before World War II, before the modernisation and the alignment with America, the toilets in temples basically consisted of a flat trough. From time to time, it was the task of the oldest monk to scratch all the filth off the walls with a wooden spade. This most unpleasant of all tasks was done by the monk who was most advanced in his practice and insight. From this also developed the koan which says that the Buddha is a shit stick. That too is Zen. Buddha is the one that has to clean out our rubbish bins. That is why it is said here: 'Why not? Pus is as pleasing to the eye as cream. Not until the truth is known does the stomach turn.' and 'verbosity is vomit.' One can observe this in psychiatry, and even in taverns. When you just let people ramble on and listen to what they are saying, it is really as if they were regurgitating.

One could demur that there are also pleasant words. Sokei-an used to require of his students that they attend two weekly Zen lectures for a year before he would give them a koan. If in the interview one presented something from the lectures, he would shout, 'Don't bring stinking philosophy into my room!' Zen is full of contradictions, it's sometimes difficult to make sense of it.

So-So continued: 'He treads the razor-edge with the agility of a fallen tree.' – Gabb's commentary to this is: 'The razor-edge of the

Middle Way is length without breadth, and may not be trodden except under illusion. The master seemingly treads this way, but for Zen the way does not exist as a thing-in-itself, and all this appeal to reasonableness, this exhortation to balance, is vanity when seen from the summit of Zen. In fact, the master has spoken no word, has taken no step. Yet a fallen tree may speak volumes to a sensitive ear, leading us far into the ineffable, as So-So himself has been led.' – Treading on the razor-edge is an old expression as a symbol for the narrow path on which one walks. One can't deviate from this path, one may look neither to the left nor to the right and allow oneself to be led astray by what is happening on the edge. One simply goes straight ahead, looking neither right nor left. That is something one really has to try and then one will notice all the many distractions that emerge from the psyche, from the ever-flowing stream of samskara. It is very difficult not to let oneself be diverted by it.

The commentary here explains that from the standpoint of emptiness even the Path of the Middle Way which the Buddha pointed out is illusory. As long as the 'I' is playing a role – *I* walk the Way, *I* strive for enlightenment – then it most certainly is illusory. There is a Zen saying, 'If you meet the Buddha, kill the Buddha.' Or, 'In front of the Buddha I bow, behind I give him a kick.' If one were to teach this kind of Zen in the West, there would probably be very few people who would take it up, because this attitude goes against the idealistic, humanistic religious outlook of many people. If one stands on the ground of idealism and humanism and doesn't know the ground of true reality, then Zen really does stink.

'In fact, the master has spoken no word. Yet a fallen tree may speak volumes to a sensitive ear.' – Sokei-an was sent to America by his teacher. He was the first living Zen master in New York and, that said, in the Western world. But before he began teaching in 1931, he lived and worked for many years in America in order to really get to know the language and the American way of thinking. One day he tripped over a dead horse that lay by the side of the road.

At that moment he had his final and definitive realisation. He immediately took the next ship to Japan to see his teacher. Thereupon he became a roshi and returned to America – There the fallen horse, here the fallen tree.

In physics class we were once asked whether a tree that falls in the forest, with no one there to hear it, makes a sound. Of course, we know that sounds only exist, when an ear is there that hears it. If there is no ear there, then the tree makes no sound.

So-So continues, 'He offends us by comparing us to babes when we still kick in the womb.' And the commentary adds: 'Ancient Taoism compared the sage to a babe, but a medieval development carried the simile back to the unborn child. Zen does not discriminate. All beings are Buddhas. So-So is trying to show his apprehension of the truth, already hinted at by the master, that the company of monks are sages in spite of their ignorance. Poor So-So, poor Master! How may they express the inexpressible? Yet try they must, for this is life.' – As I have already mentioned, on the one hand the infant is still attached to its mother's breast. On the other hand, it has come from the womb, is the original being (Urwesen) that despite its ignorance, *avidya*, is Buddha.

If one understands Zen correctly, then Tokuzan's words or Sokei-an calling us piddling infants isn't an insult. Only those who don't understand are shocked and offended.

'Poor So-So, poor Master! How may they express the inexpressible?' – The Buddha said that the great, ultimate goal is nirvana. What is nirvana? He explained nothing, he couldn't explain it. One can only experience it by stepping into nirvana. And yet the attempt must be made to speak about it. And thus one differentiates between nirvana and samsara. The world of phenomena is samsara, and nirvana is what it rests upon. In this way one tries to explain it, yet the actuality of this *ground* of samsara cannot really be explained.

So-So continued, 'He says, "No enemy under Heaven." I point to Robber Chang and Emperor Chou. He asks, "Why make plans?" I say we make plans. So-So then stepped back into his place.' Gabb's comment: 'So-So might also have pointed to children playing a game of make-believe. The game is very real to them, but do we laugh at them and try to bring them back to sense? The plans of the reformer are analogous to the play of a child, right and proper at a certain stage of development, fatuous at another. But who shall discriminate between adult and child in the assessment of values?' – Everyone should honestly ask themselves what their values really are. Formulated a little more abstractly, the question would be: 'What is reality for me?' We are not talking about philosophical values, but about that which instinctively seems real to us and according to which we orientate ourselves. That is a very legitimate question. Instead of asking others, we should observe ourselves to see what the answer is, and what it is that answers.

'Later, Tokuzan called So-So to his room. "What have we? What do we make?" he asked. So-So gave no answer.' – the commentary adds: 'The silence of assent, the stillness of understanding.'

'"Oh, Robber Chang," murmured the Master, "do you too despoil me?"' – And here Gabb comments: 'Robber or recluse, one name is as good as another. The attainment of full enlightenment by the monk deprives the Master of the further joy of watching the flower open.' – In Zen, at least in the Rinzai School, the student has to sneak up on the master like a thief and wrest the truth from him. He has to be a good thief and enter by the back door, he may never come in by the front door. If the master then complains, 'You are like a thief who has crept in through the back door and robbed me,' that is a compliment.

Today I have shown you the side of Zen which could be described as mean and shocking. If a person approaches Zen earnestly, not with hesitation or to just give it a try, then this meanness is seen as something beneficial. It is like a horrible tasting medicine. It really tastes vile, but it heals. It may be that this side of Zen is difficult for you to digest, or that what is thrown in your face makes you recoil. But what is it really that is making you shrink back?

Zen is a way that does not exist at all. What kind of way is it that doesn't even exist? You are the way, no one else, nothing else, only you yourself.